WRITING LETTERS THAT SELL:
YOU, YOUR IDEAS, PRODUCTS & SERVICES

WRITING LETTERS THAT SELL:
YOU, YOUR IDEAS, PRODUCTS & SERVICES

by Patrick Monaghan

Fairchild Publications, Inc., New York

Copyright © 1968, by Fairchild Publications, Inc.

Second Printing, June 1970

All rights reserved. No part of this book may be reproduced in any form without permission in writing from the publisher, except by a reviewer who wishes to quote passages in connection with a review written for inclusion in a magazine or newspaper.

Standard Book Number: 87005-078-8

Library of Congress Catalog Card Number: 68-19911

Printed in the United States of America

FOR:
Florence, Mary, John, Martha
and Michael

CONTENTS

Introduction

I. How to Write One Letter—To Sell Yourself   1

The Interview Letter / Techniques for Inducing Readership / The Formula: Proposition, Justification, Close / Explain Your Reason for Writing / Landing the Interview / The Strategy of Job Letters / Timing: Key Factor in Arranging Interview / How to Follow Up a Job Letter / Suggestions for Preparing to Write / Using Local Dealers for Leverage / Capitalizing on Your "Unusual Situation" / Job Letters for College (or Experienced) Marketers / Always Write to the Department Head

The Resignation Letter   11

Departing Executives Must Know Rules / Executive Must Write—Company Will Answer / Corporation Is Party One: The Executives, Departing and Remaining, Are Others / Your Ethics / If Possible—Write Letter in Advance / Do Not Change Your Mind—Bad for Your Future / Emotion Is a Luxury When It Rules Position-Changing Behavior / Timing Announcements, So Departing Executive Does Not Hurt Himself / Do Not Act under Emotion / Check with PR Director on Personal Basis / Recent Graduates Should Resign Freely—At Their Own Risk / Be Careful on Contracts—Check Legal Aspects / Make "Final" Letter Friendly

II. The Personal Business Letter   21

Formula for Effective Consumer Letters / Lead with Your Strongest Proposition / Know Your Prospect / Letters: A Retailer's Most Flexible Sales Promotion Opportunity / Writing to Neighbors: Use Your Brand Identity / Exercise Taste in Selecting Stationery / Personal Fund Raising Letters / Elements and Motives in Personal Business Fund Appeals / Letters "Break the Ice"—They Don't Close the Sale / Tailor Your Letters to Fit Specific Marketing Needs

III. How to Write One-Shot Letters to Sell the "Specialty"   30
—The Uncommon Service

Evaluate Your Special Market Need / Planning Rules for Business Letters / Pre-Writing Make Ready for a Singleton—A One-Shot / Timing: the One-Shot's Biggest Hazard / The Job of One-Shot Letters Is to Get the Order / Meet Your Objective: Relate to Reader Needs and Habits / Company-to-Company Singletons / One-Shot Opportunities in Industry and Retailing / Avoid Enclosures / Using the One-Shot in a Special Retail Situation / Economical Aspects of Single Specialty Letters

IV. **How to Estimate the Value of Your Proposition in Planning Letters to Customers and Strangers** — 40

Planning Personal Business Letters / Your Proposition Carries Impact through Motivation / Department Store Mailing Programs / Management Policy Letters—Short Cut to Stimulating Dealer Interest / The Vital Factor: Respect Your Reader's Pre-Knowledge / Establishing Strong Reader Appeal in Consumer Letters / Omit the Obvious in Company-to-Company Letters / Effective Elements in Management Policy Letters / Introducing New Models to Dealers and Customers / A Reliable Retail Image Endorses Personal Sell Letters / Propositions for Immediate or Long Term Action / Retail, Commercial and Civic Personal Business Letter Propositions / "Inside Information" Letters to Dealers and Customers

V. **Further Notes on Estimating the Value of Your Proposition in Planning Letters to Customers and Strangers** — 50

Planning New Product or New Service Letters / Larger to Smaller Company Letters / Small Company Executives Writing Large Company Executives / President-to-President Letters to Introduce "Unknowns" / Reasons for Writing / Sizing Up Your Market / Personalizing Letters / When to Direct Sales Proposals to Company Buyers / Analyzing Your Mailing List / Letter Body Describes Your Proposition / Re-Cast Letters to Meet Different Volume Factors / Your Letter Close Motivates Action / Appraise Your Follow-Up Steps / Setting Up Your Letter—Define Your Proposition in One Sentence

VI. **How to Go about the Letter Body Justification—Credibility—Timing** — 61

Rhetorical Questions Lose Readers / Justifying Your Proposition: Strength in Restraint / Finding Your Strongest Justification / Substantiating the Proposition / How a Small Company Justified Giant Corporation Consideration / The Rule in Writing Stranger Decision-Makers / Credibility Comes with the "Catch" / Letter Content, Properly Directed, Is What Sells / Timing Mailings for Sales Slow-Downs and Peaks / Always Stress Quality / Letters to Overcome Negative Situations / Prove Your Claim / Letter Acceptance Problems / Techniques for Known and Unknown Mailers

VII. **The Letter's Close** — 71

The Close Is the Beckoning Arm / The Close Tells Readers How to Handle Your Job-Seeking Proposition / Techniques in Closing Personal Business Letters: Ask for the Order / One-Shot Letters to Consumers and Companies / Closing Letters to Top Executives / Your Close Classifies Your Reader / Targets of Door-Opening Letters / Closing Commercial Letters to Retailers / Avoid Justifying in Your Close / Closing Company-to-Company Letters / When to Enclose Printed Literature / The Close Is the Work Assignment / Fund Raising Letters / Another Look at Executive Employment Letters / Summarizing the Letter's Close

VIII. **Letters to Get Business for Smaller Retailers and Service Stores** 79

Capitalizing on Personal Relations Opportunities / Letters to Re-Establish Over-Due Account Customers / How to Attract Infrequent Customers / Potential of Letters to Build Business: The Travel Agency / Motivating New Markets by Personal Service and Letters / Personalized Process Letters / Dealing with Merchandising Shortages / Letters to Handle Custom Model Shortages

IX. **The Short Letter with the Strong Proposition** 89
The Inter-Office Memo

History of the Office Memo / Advantages of the Memo for Effective Communications / Short Consumer Letters Carry a Specific Offer / Value Your Respected Name / Techniques and Taboos in Effective Short Letter Writing / The Power of Leverage in Commercial Letters / Specialized Business Letters / Handling Customer Inquiries / Keep Up-to-Date on Company and Competitive Activities / Getting Interviews with One Paragraph Letters / Separate Product and Service in Selling Letters / Emphasize a Single Element in Brief Letters to Customers / The Bargain Letter—A One-Shot Situation

X. **Your Personality in the Business Letter** 98

Fit Your Ideal Professional Image / Personality in Consumer Letters / Language Creates Reader Impressions / Determine a Writer-Reader Relationship for Impact / Constructing President-Status Letters / Organize and Research "Proposition" Memos / Assemble Use Data and Trade Information / Procedure in Project-Letters / Inserting Personality—How Should a President Sound? / The Proposition: Essential to Establishing Personality / Reflect Sender's Occupational Interests / Executive Levels Always Address Counterparts / Elements in Personality Business Letters / Value of Personalized Letters in New Product Introductions / Planning Letters in Series / Effective Written Ideas Depend on Word Personality

XI. **The Letter to the Employees** 108

Covering Touchy Relationships and Telling the Company Story / The Situation Determines the Signature / Employee Letters Are Often Defensive / Letters Where Unions Exist / A Letters Program Shows Management's Interest / Letter Opportunities: Rumors, False Reports, Job Changes / Planning Letters to Establish Acceptance / Timing: Nerve Center of Employee Letters / Secondary Readers: Major Target of Employee Letters / Letters to Salaried and Hourly Workers / Letters to Announce Changes / Letters to Employees

Being "Laid Off" / Letters to Ease Fears of Workers Not "Laid Off" / Writing Employees at Home / Offsetting Employee Fears / Using Competition to Create Better Office Morale / Letters to Salary People / Resist Publicizing Automated Equipment / Industrial Relations for Good Communications / Good Situations for Employee Letters

XII. Letters to Stockholders 123

Presenting a "Growth" Image / Acquisition Situations / Establish a Frequency Pattern for Stockholder Letters / A Viewpoint Philosophy: A Recurring Theme Line / Chief Executive Signatures to Indicate Personal Interest / Techniques in Planning Stockholder Letters / Steps in Constructing Stockholder Letters / Welcoming New Stockholders / Avoid Advance Information Disclosures / Economic Forecasts—Best Left to Meetings or Reports / Treat Stockholders as Owners / Padding the Letter's Body and Close / Confine Letters to Pertinent Matters / Handling Defensive Situations / Merger Opportunities: Spell Out the Facts / The Stockholders Relations Aspect of Public Relations

XIII. Department Store Personalized Letters 133
Note: Enclosures vs. Letters

Effectiveness of Enclosures: Few Result in Sales / New Situations in Large Store Merchandising / Increasing Appeal of Department Store Services / Suburban Shifts and Discount Stores Affect Customer Loyalty / Personalized Letters to Strengthen Quality Image / Planning Personalized Letters to Upper Income Homes / Defining Quality Position / Strategy of "Unexpected" Letters / Achieving Store Prestige / Values in Stocking Luxury Lines / Materials and Size of Personalized Letters / Make a Concrete Offer / Preparation and Composition of Selling Letters / Your Letter Body Validates Your Offer / The Close Tells Receiver What to Do Next / Personalized Letter Writing Procedures / Promoting the Store's Unique Attributes / Letters to Young Marrieds

XIV. Dealers' Customer Relations 145
The Sales Letter on Service

Commercial Letters Fortify Dealer Reputations / Letters for Quality Store Follow-Up on Sales / President-Status Letters to Customers / Timing Follow-Up Letters / President Letters to the Service Group / How to Construct Sales Follow-Up Letters / Service Propositions Before the Sale / "Unexpected" Letters to Aim at the Next Purchase / Letters to Follow-Up Service Calls / Consumer Motivation in Dealer, Department Store, and Discount Store Shopping / When to Launch Letter Programs

XV.	**The Personal Letter—In Business** **The Case for the Thank You Note for a Job-Seeking Appointment** Timing Thank You Letters / Objectivity Is the Thank You Letter's Strength / Personal Notes—When in Doubt, Send One / Letters Related to Job Changing / Professional Management Opportunities and the Rise of "Head Hunters" / Never Send a Résumé First / Letters: Number One Method to Initiate a Job Change / Unemployed Executive Letters / Techniques for Job Interview Letters / Address the "Right" Man / Sources of Executive Jobs / Executive Search Organizations / Employment Agencies / Business Page Display Advertisements / Developing a Résumé / When to Write Executive Personnel Officers / As a Rule, Always Write Department Head First / Save Your Résumé for Interviews—Make It a Closer	154
XVI.	**How to Decide Which Officer to Address** President-to-President Letters: When to Send Them / Letters to Unfamiliar Companies / Reaching the Right Executive / Commercial Letters Between Large Companies / President-Status Letters Fit Most Situations / Assembling Specialized Executive Mailing Lists / Problems in Locating "Functional" Executives / Mis-Directed Letters / Planning Commercial Letters—Using Service Agencies / Direct Mail Advertising Agencies / Learning Names and Titles / Senders Always Address Counterparts: V.P. to V.P. / Locating Strategic Receivers and Markets / Letters in Diversification Situations / Established Supplier Letters to Presidents—Avoid Enclosures / Getting the Purchasing Agent on Your Side / Following-Up Your Letters with Appointments: Who Sees Who?	164
XVII.	**Most Business Letters Lack Perspective** **Some Things to Avoid** Gimmicks, Clichés and the "Friendly Bit" Must Go / Questions, Questions, Questions / Avoid Using Commercial Letterheads to Top Men / No Stoppers, Please / Omit Cute or Wise Quotes / Some Consumer Letters Have License / Avoid Overworking Your Letter / Do Not "Visit" in Business Letters / Omit "Guessing" Prospect's Value / Be Aware of Recipient's Sex: Man or Woman? / "Flattery Will Get You No Place" / The Price Is Part of the Proposition / Avoid Appeals to "Have More Fun" / Do Not Depend Upon Your Customers / Omit: "Everybody's Doing It" / Do Not Confuse Market with Motivation / Avoid Talking About Health / Do Not Anticipate Your Reader's Response / Never Attempt to Guess Product Appeal / Do Not Depend Upon Letters for Non-Accepted Products / Do Not Overestimate an Unknown Company Name / Omit Mention of High Quality Service / Omit Standard Sales Literature with Engraved Letterhead / Do Not "Change Pace" in Act Now Close / Avoid the Original: Embrace the Fresh But Simple Way	174

INTRODUCTION

This book is for everyone who wants to improve his business letters. He may have a specialized need such as a sales manager or promotion writer in a large company trying to open doors or introduce a new line, or an association executive jogging members for better meeting attendance, or he may be in a business or profession with limited needs.

Our objective is to isolate and identify the elements of effective letters. The major types of letters themselves can be grouped this way:

> Personal business letters
> Consumer letters
> Commercial letters

The personal business letter is addressed to a specific individual and signed by another, bearing a message that is meaningful to the sender or to both. Usually dictated and typed as single letters, these also may be personalized for mailing lists over the signatures of officers whose title is calculated to be influential. This category includes personalized letters to groups addressed individually such as employees and stockholders and members of formal groups such as associations. Printed enclosures in these letters generally are confined to one piece.

The consumer letter usually is not personalized and is addressed "Dear Friend." It typically is sent to home prospects or users of products on the manufacturer's or dealer's letterhead, and encloses brochures, folders or redemption coupons. The extensive mailing list, and the minor import of the writer's or receiver's names, sets these apart from the other business letters.

The commercial letter is the multiple letter, usually personalized to an executive by function and signed by the departmental head he would deal with: sales managers to buyers, or to office managers; presidents to presidents. These invariably carry brochures, specification sheets or product folders, and in larger companies, unless the letter is impressive looking, mail clerks or secretaries divert them directly to functional departments.

Those three broad classifications are largely for easy reference in our discussions. We group as Personal Business Letters all those involving individuals, sometimes in their business or professional guise and sometimes unrelated to vocation.

The term "personalize" refers to letters reproduced in quantities with the salutation—name and address of recipient—typed in individually, and the signature forged by hand or actually signed. Our personal business category includes these when there is a personal element involved, such as shareholder, or employee. However, large-company letters to dealers, unless signed by an officer, are typical commercial letters and usually enclose their capacity of literature. Consumer letters refer only to letters from companies to prospects represented on a mailing list. The gray area here may be letters from dealers addressed "Dear Neighbor": these would be personalized unless they were sent city-wide, with enclosures, by a big store or chain.

There is a basic formula that effective business letters must follow. Except where professional or vocational considerations suggest otherwise, all business letters should be started by a statement of the proposition. Regardless of other attributes, all effective business must have a good proposition: that is the soul of the letter. The proposition should be clearly stated at the letter's outset. The objective of all letters should be to make a sale: product, service, idea or oneself. So it starts out by saying what is for sale, and under what attractive conditions. The second paragraph is the letter's body and should explain the proposition to justify favorable action. After this you should ask for the order; tell the recipient how and where to buy it.

The method of the book is to suggest a situation that might employ a letter, draft an example, then check each point as we suppose it would strike the reader. Our first example suggests the technique applied to job-seeking for management positions. This gives us an immediate opportunity to suggest a technique for preparation before writing a letter. It has another difference from most personal business letters: it is not a step, nor phase of a process, such as a marketing project, preceded and followed by other steps. The self-selling personal business letter has as its counterpart in commercial letters the "one-shot" letter aimed at selling a specialty.

The important part in planning your proposition is to identify its specific objectives. When you know exactly what the letter is aimed at doing: write that down. Unclear objectives are frequent culprits in letter failures. When a seasoned executive is thinking of changing employers he should devote an evening to preparing a skeleton outline of his background and capabilities. As a résumé this gives him a map: the high spots are the elements of his proposition. That same technique of listing values should be the preparatory phase for letters for products, services or ideas (funds, memberships, etc.).

That approach to the letter's starting point should result in an economical proposition, subject only to one further precautionary measure: before starting to write, you should form a clear judgment, or estimate, of the recipient's pre-knowledge of your subject matter. If you write: "I am writing to offer you a new color TV set for $100" your letter would lack credibility. Any offer or other proposal in a letter must show an understanding of your recipient's past relationships to your company, to similar products, and to the present market. In our considerations of specific situations requiring letters, we repeatedly refer back to this pre-knowledge factor.

Considerable attention is given to the long letters that are increasingly popular among some successful letter writers. These two-, three- and four-page letters—simulated print jobs—starting "Dear Member" (or neighbor, friend, etc.) are often from publishers who have highly qualified lists of book club members who also are "readers." Credit clubs, travel groups and social club mailing lists will read about and buy services related to hobbies, special interests and avocations. For consumer or commercial letters to strangers two pages is about the maximum: these invariably have accompanying attractive brochures, folders, etc.

This introduction will give you some idea of our approach to writing effective business letters. When viewed as segments of marketing programs their elements required to do their communicating jobs are fairly clear. When they are "one-shots" to sell they must be just as carefully fitted. And when one letter is being sent for a business objective, its elements should be equally well fitted.

We've already said you must have a good proposition before writing. Now we add another word of caution to the would-be letter writer: Don't write any kind of letters unless the recipient has visible qualifications as being your market; this, however, would not apply to redemption offers, new model announcements, invitations, or other saturation consumer mailings.

WRITING LETTERS THAT SELL:
YOU, YOUR IDEAS, PRODUCTS & SERVICES

CHAPTER I

HOW TO WRITE ONE LETTER —TO SELL YOURSELF

The self-selling, job-seeking letter is the toughest to write that most of us ever take on. As candidates for supervisory or management positions, we are usually above simple modesty, but when we try to describe ourselves, we are all thumbs.

Your first preparatory step should be to list your attributes and data: age, schooling, family status, experience, etc. For working purposes try to keep this to a single page that shows every item at a glance. Even though you may have had ten employers in five years, you lack perspective on yourself. So, after listing your qualifications, think about your reader. You must envision his point of view. Then number your ingredients. What is the Number One *reason for reading your letter*? Isolate the four or five elements that will clarify a first objective: to get a personal interview. This should be your proposition and it should be stated as the letter's opening paragraph.

THE INTERVIEW LETTER

Although few job-seeking executives use the interview letter to a top officer, its elements are often a classic example of effective personal business letters that sell. Regardless of age or experience, when writing for a management position, write only to the officer who heads the company's activities in your functional field: marketing, finance, engineering, etc. Applicants for these positions often are expected to have college degrees, but company officers seldom disqualify a candidate on that ground. Unless your credentials are highly conventional (college degree, big company experience) do not approach any personnel people until you have been interviewed by an officer, unless for an "advertised job." Decide your attitude on moving before writing and then mention it near the end of your letter.

TECHNIQUES FOR INDUCING READERSHIP

Never send a résumé to an officer until he asks for it. Use résumés on professional placement executives and personnel men.

Now that we have our numbered attributes, we are ready for the first draft. Keep this in mind: do not think only of yourself. What will induce your reader (a very busy man without time for much reading) to read your second sentence and on down? You are trying to keep your letter alive. Unless a letter to an officer clearly shows him why he should handle the matter, he will route it to Personnel for handling.

A final preparatory admonition: in all business letters what you omit may be what will make the letter work. When in doubt about a factor, omit it. Under the term reader's pre-knowledge, we discuss this essential safety valve in many of the business letter discussions to follow. Awareness of pre-knowledge might be illustrated by an association executive writing for a position with an electric association giving as a reason: "Electricity is the coming thing." Among insiders he should omit that.

THE FORMULA: PROPOSITION, JUSTIFICATION, CLOSE

In forming your proposition, the climax is telling exactly what you want. This element, restated to suit context, is also in the close. Let us try a specimen. You are in the wholesale automotive equipment field located in Cleveland, Ohio, fifty miles from Akron. For application letters below officership level, locations up to 100 miles are the practical limit unless you are moving to the reader's city for other reasons. The first step toward writing is obtaining the full name and title of the officer. Trade magazines are good sources, or you may ask any substantial appearing dealer, disclosing your intention.

W.A. Jackson
Vice President, Marketing
Good Rubber Company
Akron, Ohio

Dear Mr. Jackson:

Proposition:

At the suggestion of a Good Rubber dealer here, I am writing to ask for a personal interview leading to consideration for employment in your marketing department. My qualifications include seven years of experience related to rubber products in the automotive field for a parts distributor here, leading to my present position as supervisor of city sales.

Justification:

My age is 31; married; one child. I am a high school graduate; served in the Army two years, with an honorable discharge as Pvt. 1st class. I joined Apex Parts seven years ago as an order filler. Five years ago, I enrolled as an evening student at State University here. Studying marketing subjects, I have completed 12 credit hours, comparable to a two-year course. My motivation for enrolling was learning that Good Rubber, and others, enroll marketing trainees mainly through college campus solicitations. I feel my experience and studies would largely supplant that training. My present assignment includes handling adjustments involving correspondence. I am available immediately in the Akron-Cleveland area, and am willing to re-locate anyplace.

Close:

If your personal time limtitations would not permit you to interview me, I should like to tell my story to whatever associate you suggest. I will be available at your convenience.

EXPLAIN YOUR REASON FOR WRITING

Job-seeking letters often disclose more to practiced readers than intended. It is always good strategy to say, or sharply indicate, why you are writing to him. Normally, officers screen candidates through personnel. Your mention of his dealer in your proposition is not name-dropping. Company officers always have a little time for a dealer. That proposition includes a strong identification with automotive equipment marketing. Equally important: it properly omits mention of education in a proposition. Use it later to avoid implying that you learned his business in night school.

LANDING THE INTERVIEW

Assuming that your proposition interests Mr. Jackson, its supporting information must justify his seeing you. He learns that you are a high school graduate with seven years in a parts distributorship, and at 31 you have been through military service and pursued learning in evening school. The critical point here is that you have only a high school diploma. He knows that the personnel office might disqualify you. Many large companies tour campuses for graduates; lesser-qualified applicants may not be accepted by personnel for an executive interview.

While an officer may seldom requisition candidates for positions on an education basis, many of them are satisfied with the practice. Being non-college puts the emphasis on experience as the basis of your capability. Mr. Jackson's secretary will be your first reader. She too is non-college, so you have a friend. Her rule is to relegate non-essential mail to departments or staff, but your letter shows that you should talk to Mr. Jackson. It gets a place in the letters to the inner sanctum.

The letter's close is the quickest way you can bow out. It tells the reader how or where to get the offering. It does not add to his motivation. If he is not sold by then, forget it. He is still reading only if he is interested.

That does not mean that the close is superfluous. You can blow everything there, but you can't add "sell." It should refer back to the proposition. Your reference to his personal busy-ness is not lost on him. Buttering up an officer is bad; but if you assume he is busy, he will plead guilty.

THE STRATEGY OF JOB LETTERS

Job letters have a longer success history for management positions than any other personally motivated approach. Hundreds of executives annually reach a point where they want a change, and forthwith send off a letter to an acquaintance in another company—sometimes a competitor. The majority of these are at the "visible" level in marketing or engineering and their reasons for wanting a change are more often "climate" than economic.

Our job letter considerations are aimed at all levels, from supervisor to officership. The letter to an officer can leap-frog a possible handicap related to non-college. However, woe is he who can't indicate some seminars, special studies or other signs that he is not an out and out bootstrapper.

The basic strategic element in letters to company officers is the use of leverage—a dealer's name for example. Also, as a strategy, the element to support the proposition (interview) is that the candidate does NOT have a degree. That justifies the officer personally seeing him. If you put yourself in his position, you realize he does not want to shut the door on a sincere applicant because he lacks a college degree.

Those are strategic techniques. They should be present in all business letters. Instead of bubbling adjectives, a smattering of "reader benefit" is the basic ingredient in letters to sell.

TIMING: KEY FACTOR IN ARRANGING INTERVIEW

When your answer suggests, "See Mr. Smith, in our personnel department," the chances are you have lost. When it suggests, "See Mr. Jones, my staff assistant," you have a live one. But, if time passes and you receive no reply, that brings up another consideration: timing. When important decisions hang, time passes slowly. In job-changing situations we forget that the other fellow had a full schedule when your letter arrived. To properly estimate this aspect of timing, you should write down a date before you send your letter, giving a reasonable date when you should expect an answer. You will see the noted date is very slow in arriving. Also, in timing your letter you should avoid writing in December when year-end pressures mount. Good timing includes watching his industry's convention calendar: avoid such dates.

HOW TO FOLLOW UP A JOB LETTER

When your allotted time has elapsed and you have no answer, place a call to his office and ask to speak to his secretary. Tell her your name and say, "I sent a letter to Mr. Jackson last month. I wonder if you would know if he has had time to see or acknowledge it?" Secretaries of officers in medium or larger companies usually remember personal letters reaching them for executive jobs. Such letters may be relayed to a retained organizational consulting firm which runs confidential check-ups. Since these consultants are available to all companies for assignments, they carefully shield identifications in investigations. But that often explains delays in answers to executive job-seekers. Let us look at an example of a letter from a 40-year-old executive who wants to change from one employer to another in the paper industry. His preparations are the same as for our first example. Here is his proposition:

> Edward Jones, Vice President, Marketing
> Dakota Paper Company
> Chicago, Illinois
>
> Dear Mr. Jones:
>
> Acting upon the suggestion of a board member of my present employer, I am writing to ask for a personal interview to discuss consideration for a position in your organization. My present position is Eastern sales manager, Federal Paper Company, a position I have held for three years, after numerous posts leading to it over seven years since I joined Federal.
>
> My reason for wishing to change is entirely related to a personality conflict of several years standing that appears unlikely to be resolved. My age is 40 years; married, two teen-age children. My education is high school diploma; the equivalent of two years of college level marketing courses, and fifteen years marketing experience in the paper industry. Prior to joining Federal, I was a junior district specialist for. . . . . .

Here the board member qualifies as your leverage. In view of the competitive aspects, it is logical that you would not name him. That reference suggests some relationship at that level; enough for the executive to read your proposition. This type of proposition—between competitors—must depend more upon its justification than upon itself. Your profile must make you sound attractive.

That specimen supplies a logical reason for seeing you, but it also implies a well organized approach. Let us look at a brief and elemental letter outline:

1. It identifies and sets up our proposition with a strong reference at the outset.
2. It describes us briefly, aimed at saying why that company, and why that officer.
3. It asks for the order. It makes the reader decide to see us or arrange for an associate to do so.

The close is the same as our other example. Offers to see him, or an associate. Busy executives, who delegate everything possible, also measure everything to determine what *not* to delegate. The fact that you are not a routine job-seeker sustains interest; but you must ease conditions for the interview. The board member's identity should not again come up.

SUGGESTIONS FOR PREPARING TO WRITE

Some good marketing executives, from recent trainees to key men near the top, move on to new positions many times as a matter of course. Figures show that in marketing approximately 75 percent of all top executives are in their second, third or fourth job. Twenty percent came up through the ranks and never moved. Five percent are college graduates who joined firms right after school.

The personal letter to the head of marketing (or finance, engineering or whatever your chosen field) is almost always an effective way of approaching any company you would like, but for such letters to succeed they must be carefully thought out from the desired company's viewpoint.

As a distributor's sales manager, you may hear that a company nearby is scouting for someone with your experience. In evaluating your situation with a friend, he may verify that Good Rubber Company is looking for a sales manager. Jackson, the vice president of marketing, is a fine executive. "Really has a good program." Your first stop might be at the public library, where you can examine the statistical profile of Good Rubber Company. Also, verify the names of all officers and directors. Jackson's name will be there and you will learn whether he is on the board.

USING LOCAL DEALERS FOR LEVERAGE

It may sound elemental, but you should look in the yellow pages to identify Good's dealer, name and location. Unless you have uncovered a better way, introduce yourself to the dealer with the statement that a family member bought some Good Rubber stock and asked you about it. Identify yourself by name and company. Unless the dealer is new with Good, he will know quite a bit about the company, especially their products and product plans. He may even know Jackson. Tell him you have heard of Jackson. If he enthuses, get on the band wagon with him. You can even say, "I admire an outfit that does business that way." If the dealer does not suggest you have a talk with Jackson, you can suggest it. "Do you think he would talk to me?" you might ask. Now you are ready to compose a letter.

Dear Mr. Jackson:

At the suggestion of John Brown, your dealer here, I am writing to ask if I might impose on you for a brief personal interview. I am interested in applying for a position in marketing administration that will fully use my 12 years of field and management sales experience. I have decided to make an occupational change whenever I can locate with a company such as Good Rubber that can use my experience in the consumer or industrial fields.

I joined my present employer five years ago in the field selling organization. Fifteen months ago I was named sales manager with five regional and 12 district representatives reporting to me. Several factors not related to the marketing program have influenced my decision to move.

My age is 40; I am married with two small children. My home has been in this city since early childhood and I graduated from East High School and studied business subjects for two years at State University. Family economics caused my withdrawal from college after two years and I entered city sales for a meat packer. My present salary is $16,500. I joined the Marines in 1950 and was given a medical discharge at the end of my three-year tour.

If you could spare time to see me personally, I would greatly appreciate it. If your schedule does not permit, perhaps an associate could see me. Whatever meets your convenience would be appreciated.

                                      Yours very truly,

When you seek employment at an executive level, your present title tells a prospective employer your basic experience. But, as an employed older manager, you should give your present salary. Also, an executive should give the name of his dealer reference. Otherwise the burden of your letter is the same as in the younger man's letter.

CAPITALIZING ON YOUR "UNUSUAL SITUATION"

Good letter-writing technique is especially necessary for job-seekers with an unusual situation. These might include the fellows who have made a bad choice the first time, or graduates who have worked two years or more on a career job and want to move on. Let us try a letter for the first mentioned type. Incidentally, never write on your present employer's letterhead.

Dear Mr. Jackson:

A few weeks before graduation from Triangle State, I was interviewed on campus for a marketing position with Good Rubber Company. While I was favorably disposed, a personal matter caused me to forego the offer in favor of one in the paper industry. I now recognize that my judgment was at fault and am writing to ask if I might have an interview with you or an associate.

My age is 23; I have married since graduation. My class standing was in the top one-half, with my major in marketing. When I realized that my position choice was not what I expected, I visited the Good Rubber Company dealer near here. He advised that I write to you. I am familiar with Good Rubber quality as a user.

I have a strong interest in research and communications. In my class work my writing skills were considered well above average. Please be assured that I have no personal commitment to any specialized marketing function. Should an interview qualify me for marketing employment, I would accept whatever assignment suited the company's programs. I can be available for an interview at your convenience.

Sincerely,

The proper sign-off of business letters permits the use of "Sincerely" only on job-seeking letters. On others, the impersonal "Very truly yours" is preferable.

In this type of letter the campus solicitation is inherent in your application. If you are writing as a recent graduate who did not receive a campus offer you would qualify the statement to read ". . . I planned making a pre-graduation interview application to Good Rubber Company, but a personal matter intervened and I accepted my present position in the paper industry. . . ."

When special qualifications, such as education, experience or your personal interests qualify you for a specific department in a company, you should address that department head. It may be preferable that he is an officer of the company. In seeking marketing work, with or without experience, and the company has dealers, distributors, or suppliers, you should call on one of these. Also, there is an outside chance you may wind up going to work for one of them.

JOB LETTERS FOR COLLEGE (OR EXPERIENCED) MARKETERS

Approximately 90 percent of all employed Americans are in the market for another job, an organizational management consultant recently told the author. "Few of these are active . . . but, 'if the right offer came along . . .'." The easiest letter to write is the one from an experienced man.

> Dear Mr. Jackson:
>
> At the suggestion of a Good Rubber Company dealer of my acquaintance I am writing to ask for an interview for a position in the Good Rubber marketing department. For the past six years I have supervised market research and acted as marketing correspondent for a medium-size producer in the paper industry.
>
> In writing to you directly for an interview, my present employment is secure if your needs are not met by my qualifications; if they are, I would expect to make an application through personnel channels.
>
> My age is 32. I am married and enjoy good health. I have completed two years of Business Administration at Triangle State, and have since pursued home study courses informally. My principal reason for wishing to change jobs is that I wish to work in consumer goods, yet I feel that my extensive experience in industrial marketing would be useful.

I would appreciate an interview with you, or if you cannot spare the time, with one of your associates. Thank you for your consideration.

Sincerely,

Letters such as this specimen are invariably well-received if the recipient is in the market for a specialist. If you write it from your home address, it is not a violation of employer confidence.

You will observe that all of the letter specimens shown use the same formula: state the proposition; briefly supply the vital statistics (age, etc.) and imply some knowledge of the company's business. In the first specimen, rather than mention being a "user" the writer mentions ". . . consumer marketing . . . has industrial marketing . . ." that clearly shows knowledge of marketing types.

In our examples we have adhered to a stereotype in using the tire industry. The positions mentioned are common to many consumer-industrial companies that might include numerous industries in the automotive field, appliances, electronics and office equipment.

ALWAYS WRITE TO THE DEPARTMENT HEAD

A letter does not supplant a direct interview where you can see the desired executive by other means. On the other hand, in almost every position in marketing, finance, engineering, production or sub-divisions of these, an applicant for administrative or management positions should write to the department head rather than applying through personnel. He may be sent back to personnel, but he is better off if he can apply through the department head.

The Resignation Letter

DEPARTING EXECUTIVES MUST KNOW RULES

In a widely shown movie during the Great Depression, Charles Laughton was portrayed as a bedevilled office clerk of little hope. One day, when things were darkest, a letter arrived revealing that he had inherited a fortune. With not a moment's hesitation, still holding the glad letter in his hand, he burst into the inner sanctum. Before his astounded superior could ask, "What's the meaning . . . ?" clerk Laughton pursed his lips and let out a raucous "razzberry"—audible throughout the acres of desks behind him—then he backed out, slammed the door and grabbed his hat without pausing as he left.

That theatrical bit is a fairly obvious luxury, but only relatively more so than the executive who stands on "dignity" or "principle" and tells his superior to get another boy.

The same care and thought should go into terminating a position, that goes into securing it. And management owes equal consideration to its terminations. Recruiting and enrolling, when used to successfully build, are highly valuable; firing and losing executives is costly to every employer. But probably the employee, when he is an executive, stands to lose the most when he changes jobs. If he stands to gain he must be doubly correct.

EXECUTIVE MUST WRITE—COMPANY WILL ANSWER

As a bread and butter matter, both companies and individuals should write termination letters for the record. Taxes, insurance, liability and property are invariably involved immediately, but where no record is mutual, embarrassments and misunderstandings can crop up a year later. The letter should always "regretfully resign" in one form or another. Never write a letter conceding that you were discharged. You should always resign and show it that way in the employer's records. If you do that and receive an acknowledgment letter, that will constitute your testimony after the individuals involved are not present. If an executive departs from a position without a written statement of "friendly parting," any jealous rival can fabricate a damaging story and it is difficult to refute. So: always submit a resignation letter when you terminate.

CORPORATION IS PARTY ONE: THE EXECUTIVES, DEPARTING AND REMAINING, ARE OTHERS

An executive employed by a company is one of a three-party understanding. His superior (or personnel executive) is another; and the

Company is the Number One part. The Company retains its status quo no matter what happens; the manager keeps his position, the record and the budget. The departing executive leaves alone. If he coolly submits to The Company, to the attention of the Manager, a gracious letter, he will receive a warm reply. We are assuming that approximately one half of departures are firings. It may be a sense of destiny, but few surviving managers want ill will among the "alumni."

YOUR ETHICS

Ordinary fine points of ethics do not apply in matters where you must protect your family's living. The letter you write perhaps would be most honest if it said: ". . . you slave driver . . ." but wisdom would dictate ". . . under your wise leadership . . . ." It should never mention another employee, supplier or dealer. Your highest ethics are what will best serve your career. It is assumed that the executive is not guilty of malfeasance. Regardless of the attitude of management, an executive who has done his best is entitled to a high recommendation when he leaves, whatever the reason. His means of getting that is the resignation letter: and its answer.

IF POSSIBLE—WRITE LETTER IN ADVANCE

Most often, executives resign because they have already accepted another position. Under such circumstances, the letter should be written, pocketed, and an appointment requested. Do not disclose your intention. If your relationship with your superior has been on a strictly business basis, the interview should be kept brief and businesslike. More often, personal relationships exist among executives. That should not change your story, but it would imply: "we remain friends." Never make a resignation statement on any tentative basis. In fact, when you reveal your intention verbally, you should not name the future employer, and under no circumstances should you mention or hint regarding your new economics. In instances where executives— one reporting to another—are on close social terms, the resignation will not often come as a surprise. Executives who socialize usually share whatever they please—including overtures from other companies.

DO NOT CHANGE YOUR MIND—BAD FOR YOUR FUTURE

A final pre-letter admonition: If you walk in to resign: resign. Do NOT accept an increase instead, unless the entire upheaval is related to abnormal conditions such as ". . . one of us must go . . . ." After you have stated your business, expressed regrets and offered "cooperation" in departure, you should place the enclosed letter on his desk and shake hands: then go.

A typical resignation letter, as follows, is in good taste. Written on your personal stationery, preferably with home address:

Jones Manufacturing Company
New York, N.Y.

Attention: John Jones,
President

Gentlemen:

With deep personal regret, I am tendering my resignation of employment to be effective March 1, 19—. A business opportunity has been presented to me, by a Company not related to the fields served by Jones Company, that has benefit potentials highly advantageous to me and to my family.

During my service with the Company I have enjoyed the most cordial relationships with all fellow members of management and with the others in the organization. Also, I have the highest respect for the operational course and policies of the company as they affected my assignment.

Subject to your acceptance and agreement with my proposed termination date, I shall proceed to assist you or whomever you assign to transfer my present duties without interrupting their flow. Also, I shall ask the Personnel Department to process whatever papers may be necessary; including the return of my Company identification, credit and other such property.

Please be assured that I stand ready to fully cooperate on all matters for mutual convenience.

Best personal regards,

Sincerely yours,

Edward Brown
Vice President—Marketing

In assessing that our specimen may be somewhat saccharine, you must bear in mind that in five or ten years Mr. Jones may be gone. Meanwhile, it is aimed partially at inspiring an answer. When you have Mr. Jones' response, you attach the two. When you submit an application—now or at a later time—you can enclose Xerox copies. Please note ". . . opportunity presented . . . not in Jones' field . . . advantageous. . . ." Do not say in a formal resignation letter: "I have accepted. . . ." It smacks of job seeking on the Company's time; and it may cause ill feelings. However, only rarely should any executive resign any position before he has another. Executives normally carry a higher price tag, for another employer, when they are employed, than when found on the beach. Also, some companies avoid hiring non-employed.

A majority of job-shifting executives remain in their present industries. If your new situation is such, you still omit mention of industry or employer in your letter. On a social basis, you are not under that restraint.

EMOTION IS A LUXURY WHEN IT RULES POSITION-CHANGING BEHAVIOR

In some industries when an executive resignation is announced, unless it is accompanied or followed very soon by an announcement of a new position of equal or better standing, the assumption is that the executive was fired. It should be the rule of all executives: "I will never be fired. Not only are there no figures on self-motivated vs. forced departures, but even those who are "separated" can manage to rationalize that the company lacked flexibility. Regardless of reasons, or actual circumstances, emotion should be kept out of executive job termination situations. If a superior is making a poorly concealed effort to inspire a "resignation," rather than becoming upset, executives should be scheming on the content of their resignation letter. It may not always be realistic to say nothing in self-defense, but most executives agree, when discussing "separating an employee," that they never reconsider when they hear his "argument." Almost without exception, once a termination interview starts, it is final.

Most executives are not surprised if caught in a termination situation, because both parties have the same facts. The employer-executive is seldom surprised when a top-performer quits. He knows he can lose the attractive performers. He will seldom try to dissuade the executive from his intention.

TIMING ANNOUNCEMENTS, SO DEPARTING EXECUTIVE DOES NOT HURT HIMSELF

Whatever else he says, if an executive is "terminated" he should convey, "you read my mind. I resign. And I will submit my letter within the hour."

That may sound slightly like an old vaudeville blackout. It is actually a long-sighted way of terminating executive employment. And very few employers will repeat, "You're terminated." If you knew things were bad, you have a letter in your locked desk drawer. When it has been submitted, sit down and prepare a calendar announcing your change.

DO NOT ACT UNDER EMOTION

Timing is of the essence in building your personal image, or prestige, in job-changing. Here are the steps:

If your termination came suddenly, you would have not submitted your resignation letter yet. If you must compose it, tell your superior you will drop it off in the morning. Take it home for careful handling. Two ways of opening (on these quick terminations) are equally good:

"In keeping with our discussion I herewith am formally submitting my resignation. As you know, it is with great personal regret that I take this action, which I wish to be effective at the first of next month, or whenever sooner is convenient for the company. . . ."

The other preferred form (for quick after-discussion use):

"With deep personal regret I wish to submit my resignation to become effective on the first of next month, or any earlier date that meets your convenience.

"It is my pleasure to report that the programs and projects of my office are in shipshape; and all key positions are in capable hands. Whoever is chosen as my successor will find a full corps of willing and able staff people. . . ."

Those openings meet two "quick" situations: If the superior is friendly, use the "In keeping with . . . ." If he is reserved about "accepting" a resignation, open the letter directly ". . . submit my resignation . . . effective . . . ." Your copies will go into your file for interviews now or at any later time.

CHECK WITH PR DIRECTOR ON PERSONAL BASIS

You probably are acquainted with the PR director. Call him and say, "I just resigned, but I do not wish to announce my new position yet. I know you do not announce resignations, but I would appreciate it if you would let me know if a successor in my position is to be announced. Then I might want to announce at the same time." PR directors are familiar with both holding up and releasing resignations. Just to be safe: tell him not to release news of your resignation. Very few large companies will announce resignations, even when asked to.

Such announcements are often taken to mean "fired."

Your next step is to write a personal letter to all of your personal friends whom you would like to have know that you are changing situations. This might include customers of your present employer, but not the "dealer list," or "suppliers." As events work out, you may not be announced in the business pages and trade magazines for a month. The letter to friends or customers should start:

". . . I am resigning my position and decided to drop a line to you and a couple of other friends, before I release it to the press.

"Details will await our next personal meeting, but I have not felt the freedom, in some respects, that permits my most effective efforts. Working with (first and last name of present superior) has been very gratifying. He is certainly an able executive. The organization here is very fine: in fact, leaving is not going to be easy.

"Some time ago I was approached on a proposition that seemed ideal in the light of my family's future. I decided to keep it on the back burner, until I decided to leave here. Either I shall go toward that, or I may hold off and take a short rest. You will hear from me again soon. . . ."

That letter is bait, and it gives those who know you an "inside position" when word circulates, "Old Joe is out . . . ." The "proposition . . ." must be invented. No one believes anyone quits a job unless he knows where he is going.

When you sign in for a new position, immediately tell your new PR director to issue a release. But call your old superior and his PR director and tell them (if they are just hiring a successor, they may ask you to hold up). Do that, but write another letter to your friends, telling them. Then in your new announcement include mention of your former position. And tell the PR there to mention that you "recently resigned."

RECENT GRADUATES SHOULD RESIGN FREELY—AT THEIR OWN RISK

Some recent data among business school graduates entering "training" programs in large companies indicated that four of ten changed positions at least once in the first two years. Most companies have personnel records showing the service terms of these recruits. One company reported that among such employees the attrition rate among "trainees" was double that among graduates assigned directly into departmental responsibilities.

The junior executive's decision to change positions is not often a surprise to employers. Even law school graduates, with career intentions, who enter big law departments in large cities suddenly decide to return to their hometowns, when their wives have difficulty negotiating the baby buggy on apartment house stairways. The only suggestion we have is that a letter of resignation be submitted for the records. It can be very simple:

> Dear Mr. Jones:
>
> Regretfully, I herewith resign my position with the Company, effective at the end of this month.
>
> My reasons for this decision are purely personal and in no way related to the Company or supervision. I joined the Company a year ago as my first employment when·graduated from State U. My

personal respect for Jones Corporation caused me to accept its proffer in accounting. After this year of experience I have concluded that my future will be in marketing. The Company I considered before joining Jones recently renewed its offer. I expect to move there.

I have greatly enjoyed the warmth and friendly feelings among members of the Jones Company. I sincerely hope that my leaving, in the best interests of my family, is not inconvenient. I will follow procedures for termination with the Personnel Department.

Thank you for your many courtesies,

Sincerely,

Here, as in all such letters, the answer, or acknowledgment, will have value as a link in your career in later years. While big companies trace out all past employment records and schooling, after five years, the only meaningful data will be in expressions of your relationships as you left employment places.

All executives at some time in their careers are faced with leaving a place of employment and resuming in a new stable. Among the most undecipherable of all grey areas of business is the complex of reasons behind many of such changes: they may be as simple as "more money for less work" or they may be results of mergers. No matter what the reasons are for job changing, a year later only your record will be potentially visible. If we were merely suggesting that you "submit a resignation" when terminated, that would not be a problem. Rather, we advocate a type of letter that says you are resigning, without including a reason and without revealing future plans. The differences between being asked to resign, or asking a company to accept your resignation are more matters of timing than fact.

BE CAREFUL ON CONTRACTS—CHECK LEGAL ASPECTS

When an executive is under contract, it may be necessary to gain company agreement before a termination is effective. You should consult your lawyer. Looming over all separations of executives is the tent that stands for the industry in which your business is operated. When you are moving from one company in an industry to another, you should always informally discuss the move with your superior before submitting any writing. As mentioned earlier, most executives deal largely with executives who are also employees.

A reason to write to the Company, Attention: J. Jones, is that at a later time it will not appear to be a personal correspondence. Mr. Jones may not be there long either. Always write any letters involving your future to the Company—not to individuals. If you report to the Board, address letters to it.

To summarize the resignation letter: its real significance is likely to be a year or more away. That suggests that any executive who plans to make a move should draft a resignation letter and have it in his personal home file. Emotion is a dangerous element in a letter and it may be difficult to avoid it, should your resignation be handled on short notice.

In our examples we always place the fact of resigning first in the shortest possible sentence. By following up immediately with ". . . I regret . . . opportunity . . ." you are framing the circumstances to appear negative to the Jones Company in losing you.

MAKE "FINAL" LETTER FRIENDLY

In letters concerned with any vital matter, the physical length is immaterial. Fluffing them slightly gives the impression of extreme fairness, on your part, in explaining a necessity. Avoid introducing any element related to the future. That is to say ". . . advantageous to me and my family" is your only implication of the future. If you even hint that you are employed by a competitor, the letter may be evidence in a later lawsuit.

Never give reasons of "health" unless you are retiring. Never say ". . . open my own office . . ." even if you have such a plan. In many instances when word circulates that an executive is leaving a company, out of a clear sky comes an offer. Everything you write will be considered legitimate "info" for talk around the clubs, etc. So supply no hints. Your friends will interpret your move favorably; but that is when the jealous show their colors.

CHAPTER II

THE PERSONAL BUSINESS LETTER

The average person, even among businessmen, does not have occasion to write many personal business letters. As an urban citizen occasionally engaged in civic or welfare chores, his writing opportunities would tend to be greater than as a consumer writing to manufacturers or stores.

Letters between companies and consumers are a one-way street to the degree that a consumer letter means one from a company to a consumer. Companies dealing in products reaching millions of consumers have customer relations departments to handle the complaints. Incoming congratulations and other good notices are likely to find their way to the executive addressed.

It is not entirely a mark of cynicism for consumers to say that letters to manufacturers are a waste of time. Not all letters. Some of the most unpleasant letters addressed to presidents reach them, especially if they start out ". . . as a stockholder in your. . . ." Most letters of complaint are composed when the product or service has failed, and they reflect more emotion than fact. These receive attention, but not more than if they were more temperate.

FORMULA FOR EFFECTIVE CONSUMER LETTERS

Our discussions here of personal business letters are from the viewpoint of the individual or consumer, but they embody the essential formula effective for commercial or consumer letters. We use the term "commercial" for business-to-business letters whose mission is sales; and the term "consumer" for company letters to users or prospects. There are numerous types of business letters written for sales, ranging from simulated print or process jobs to the personally composed and dictated letter from president to president, seeking to open a door to a salesman or to get an order through the mail.

Writing as a citizen, or as an individual composing one letter to one reader, our formula will not necessarily differ from a letter written to you as a citizen by a company or other institution. In either instance we might well start by making a simple outline. Our first consideration should be to identify for ourselves the specific objective of this letter. Sometimes the name of the recipient is itself the objective. If you have been assigned to solicit members for a new bowling league, your objective and salutation might be "Dear Fellow Bowler:" with the personal name substituted for "Fellow Bowler." You establish first that your letters go only to bowlers.

LEAD WITH YOUR STRONGEST PROPOSITION

Before starting to write or dictate you should list the ingredients of your proposition: benefits that can be embodied in the first-sentence proposition. You may have an acquaintance on your list whose recreation and work habits are known to you. You know that he bowls, but you are not familiar with his present commitments. Let us hypothecate some benefits:

1. Group made up of neighbors
2. Close to home—mainly once-a-week bowler
3. Starting time early but allowing time to reach home from office
4. Cost arrangement highly favorable
5. Members encouraged to select a team from among those not filled
6. Refreshment prices moderate, in moderate lounge
7. Withdrawal possibilities feasible because of a "fairly high rate of business transfers among neighbors"

Benefits inherent in the proposition are the essence of all selling letters. But the value of a benefit is closely related to the law of supply and demand. Here we are offering a known bowler a ready-made bowling opportunity near home among neighbors. This may not be our strongest proposition, but if it is we should place it at the head of our letter.

KNOW YOUR PROSPECT

In writing, where the initial burden is to hold a reader who has not been too difficult to reach, we should skip amenities. None of this: "... in this day and age when everyone is on the run" stuff. Even more vital is a proper analysis of your prospect's present knowledge or degree of familiarity with your field. "A game that does more for the nation's health than all the medicine ever concocted . . ." might find your prospect in agreement, but if he is a bowler he probably belongs to a league that meets his needs. Now you can sharpen your proposition, retaining the order of listing benfits, but reducing them to one or two words: 1) Neighborhood group; 2) close; 3) early start; 4) low cost; 5) choice of teams; 6) low cost refreshments; 7 interruptable.

Dear Mr. Jones:

A group of neighbors in the Claremont area are forming a bowling club essentially for those who work away from the neighborhood and miss the visiting and friendships not possible in our limited home time. We would like to invite you to join, or if you cannot now make a commitment, to be our guest when we take the Lanes at 8:30 p.m. any Thursday evening at Marigold Lanes on Central Avenue.

As you may know, Claremont has a fairly high incidence of business transfers. For that reason our members understand that they may withdraw upon relatively short notice. Most of those joining are once-a-week bowlers. Also, most express themselves as anxious to break up at a reasonably early hour.

The cost arrangement worked out with the proprietor is well within the price range of the city. The modern lounge offers refreshments at popular prices.

Should you have questions, I can be reached at home evenings (except Thursday) 867 3492. I hope you can drop around to Marigold next Thursday evening.

Best Wishes,

An important admonition to business letter-writers is: do not overlook asking for the order. Even supposing that the basic purpose of a commercial letter—for office supplies, insurance or a manufacturing tool—is to open the door for the salesman, the recipient may be waiting for someone suggesting your product or service. More to the point: if it is directed to the proper executive, your letter might bring a response more quickly than you anticipated.

LETTERS: A RETAILER'S MOST FLEXIBLE SALES PROMOTION OPPORTUNITY

As the most flexible form of promoting sales, the letter is the most neglected opportunity of retailers of all sizes. Department stores stuff monthly bills with offers; automobile, tire and gasoline dealers share the cost of factory mailings, and numerous others use product samples. The oddity of this situation is that every one of those dealers knows more about the needs and habits of their neighborhoods than a factory-hired promotion man could possibly know. In the small towns during an earlier era, merchants met their neighbors and customers coming or going to Sunday services. Nothing beats the warmth of a handshake, as your Congressman will tell you. But in cities and suburbs today, families are more remote. Yet, an authority on department store operations said recently that these stores have more accounts than a generation ago. But few of them have their eyes closed to discount and mail order chains that have become major business factors in recent years. Our subject is interested in competitive pricing only as it affects business letters. Most old-line merchants or dealers can hold forth at length on how their prices are lower, across the board, than a notorious discounter. "Notorious" is the merchant's word. His fallacy is that pricing is the discount store's home ground. Even though limited facilities make possible sending only ten processed, personalized letters weekly, no retailer is too small for that. And none is too large.

When asked, "Why don't you write some letters to your neighbors and new families?" many dealers become defensive. "We are members of the Lady Who Welcomes services. We get about a dozen of our free lubrication with oil change cards back monthly . . ." a gasoline dealer might say. Or a dry cleaner says, "We give a dollar off on all first orders from new families. We can't afford any more."

In the main, retailers do not write business letters because they haven't a feeling of sufficient skill at writing. Most retailers were attracted to Main Street operations because they liked to meet people. Few are aware of how long it is between personal encounters with neighbors and customers.

This guide is not undertaking to convince its readers that they should write letters. The way that these powerful tools are overlooked by retailers is our excuse for volunteering information outside our scope. As a specialist analyzing letter-readers' reactions to mail, we will volunteer this added encouragement to reluctant retailers who are not averse to trying some personal letters.

WRITING TO NEIGHBORS: USE YOUR
BRAND IDENTITY

Just as the gist of the personal greeting is its warmth, so is the gist of a personal business letter in its straightforwardness in offering a good proposition. Grammar is secondary. If you have the franchise for a nationally respected line of TV sets and other home electronic products, a standard brand of tires, a strong line of petroleum products, a good line of white goods, outdoor electric goods or electric housewares you should identify with that brand name in the strongest possible manner. That would be a personal letter to your neighbors.

In writing to neighbors, it is well to keep in mind that, unlike yourself, they are not privy to current situations in your field. For example, during a period when color TV was new, the industry could not supply the demand in most parts of the country. Industry surveys showed that dealers did not take advantage of the shortages. Many had been through such scarcity periods before and conducted themselves in a way that built character. It was when the shortages vanished that many dealers revealed a lack of planning for the long pull. As ample supplies reached them, many used the occasion to offer bargains and to follow up earlier disappointed shoppers. A few dealers put women on telephones telling about bargains in color TV.

A personal letter to every customer fits this situation:

Dear Mrs. Jones:

We now have Superba, the world's quality color TV leader, in a full choice of models at reduced prices. You may recall that last year, and the year previous, when a color-tube shortage caused supplies to be short and prices high, we did not urge our customers to bid at the prices. Now we are ready to offer them the finest sets at prices not above what some paid for indifferent brands.

As a neighbor you know that we operate a full-time, fully-manned factory trained service department. Before any TV set leaves our shop, it is given a thorough make-ready for installation. Even more important, we analyze each set's characteristics to match those of your room for top performance. All sets that leave here are adjusted to their location by our engineers.

If you have not as yet selected your color set, I would consider it a privilege to show and demonstrate the fine products of Superba. The prices are in line with values and you may be sure that we will continue to protect our customers in this important factor. May we see you soon?

Yours very truly,

The opening sentence in the letter says the store has Superba, a leading national brand color TV set in a full supply of choices at reduced prices. Its second paragraph starts: "As a neighbor." In the final paragraph he asks for the order by saying ". . . a privilege to show and demonstrate . . . Superba. . . ."

We must be careful not to overdo the appliance dealer's great asset: the friendly neighbor. In billboards, newspapers and radio commercials, it is difficult to overstate friendliness. In letters the note of sincerity does that. Re-stating it tends to give it a hollow ring.

EXERCISE TASTE IN SELECTING STATIONERY

Dealers for automobiles, appliances and other brand goods have a tendency to use stationery that is over-commercial. If you glance through a pile of letters, selected at random from a day's or week's mail, you will notice that the better, and larger companies tend toward black lettering on white stationery. If they carry a monogram, it too is in black—and it is tastefully small. The only reason for startling the recipient with garish stationery is to get his attention. Good names are stronger than loud ink.

In our above color TV letter, please note that reduced prices and full line of choices are in the first sentence. Those are at the top among reasons families patronize stores, so you put them at the top in your letter. Most good salesmen of the types we are discussing use a selling formula not unlike these elements—in the same order—when they approach a customer in the store or follow them up to their homes. The fact is that in selling work conducted in person, the salesman has much more latitude than in a letter. Most salesmen compulsively pass the time of day, contribute an amenity or two, before they state their business. If their first stab at getting acquainted meets impatience, they jump right to business. The meandering letter is insensitive to its precarious position—right over the waste-basket.

PERSONAL FUND RAISING LETTERS

A thorough understanding of the formula for an effective personal business letter writing capability would seem to qualify one to compose the annual appeal to fellow alumni. If we are licensed professional practitioners, letter-writing is a lesser-needed skill. But an off-setting negative is that we have professional prestige that would bruise if exposed as harboring hanging participles or split infinitives. Actually, these blots on the prideful prose of strict grammarians are not identifiable by most readers, and so it is with most grammar. Who needs it? We do if our sentence structure is faulty to the point that we are not clear. That is the extent of your need for proper grammar in the business world. In the academic world the influentials are sensitive to errors and they don't approve. This means that when a marketing executive (or another whose grammar skills are secondary) is named to go after the alumni, he should have his letter fly-specked by a faculty member before it is sent.

Let us apply our formula to a college appeal:

Dear Mr. Jones:

I recently had a call from Prexy Smith asking if I'd get together with several hundred who graduated with us and tell them the story of how Triangle State is planning to meet its operating costs and go ahead on the new gymnasium now somewhat overdue. I told him I would talk about it to a small group whose fortunes since leaving school are familiar to me. That explains my urgent request that you join some 20 or 25 others to get the full story.

I have reserved the Billings Room at the Astor for an informal luncheon Tuesday, August 24 at 12:00 noon. We have no program except that we are trying to have Prexy Smith present, but not for a speech. I am sure you will agree that if we are to get this thing off the ground some of our more visible brothers must be included. I definitely count on you as one of these. Please call Miss Joy in my office if I can count on you.

My best regards to the family,

Sincerely yours,

ELEMENTS AND MOTIVES IN PERSONAL BUSINESS FUND APPEALS

Personal business letters asking for money have two elements to hang their hat on: 1) to communicate to the expected donor that he is visible and 2) that he at least owes an obligation to attend a discussion meeting. Professional money-raisers for established welfare or health funds know that they seldom bring in a new donor. The donors are there. They use cross-lists to find them. The inevitable exception is the surprise big donation. Almost as inevitably, it turns out to come from a name on the list whose family has been afflicted by the disease involved.

None of the foregoing is of great moment to an alumni group that will collect a few thousand dollars for a college project. The workable ore here is closely related to solvency. When the group is assembled the Prexy or another self-sacrificing spellbinder tells of the need, or the competition with Old Siwash, and of Old Triangle's tradition of always coming through. We shall not pause to list the elements in the specimen letter. Among strong motives for college giving among alumni are: 1) desire to see the objective accomplished; 2) anxiety to make good in the eyes of a hero of youthful days; 3) being numbered among those alumni who are visible—having made a mark of some kind. None of these would normally bring in more than $10 or $25 donations. When he is sitting among contemporaries, he pledges $100 or perhaps $250.

LETTERS "BREAK THE ICE"—THEY DON'T CLOSE THE SALE

The purpose of the foregoing example is two-fold: 1) it attempts to apply the same formula as our initial job-seeking letter and 2) it shows that letters are not really meant to close the sale. If the letter gets the prospect to the luncheon, an experienced Development Director will take it from there. Some of these staff professionals assist with the letters. It is better all around if you write your own letter under circumstances such as these.

As a communications form, letters are one of man's oldest means of exchange. Probably because they are solidly established, their forms have rendered many specimens almost unrecognizable. But letters are among the few promotion devices used by large companies that are available in large quantities to an average citizen. Ironically, with all of their resources, many industrial and consumer giant corporations use the personal business letter far less effectively than does a precinct politician when he writes to the editor.

TAILOR YOUR LETTERS TO FIT SPECIFIC MARKETING NEEDS

As we proceed to discuss marketing requirements of various types and levels of businesses—manufacturers, distributors, dealers—we see a common pattern. In some letters the burden is to get effective action after they get the message—that is the common problem of consumer letters. They hold the letter and look at it, but they have eyes only for the redemption coupons. In other letters the problem is to land on the mail pile in the inner office of the top management to whom our letter is addressed. Once a consumer opens the mailing piece or an executive has our opened letter in his hand our mission is started toward success. In the chapters to follow we attempt to fit those situations to the marketing objectives of various types of businesses or institutions.

CHAPTER III

HOW TO WRITE ONE-SHOT LETTERS TO SELL THE SPECIALTY —THE UNCOMMON SERVICE

Every business category, and many an institution and profession, classifies its stock-in-trade according to commodities and specialties. Each has its bread and butter lines that support the business and each has some relatively low-volume, limited appeal, non-repeating items, or items that always fall just short of established demand. These are their specialties.

Retailers have a very real need to understand selling by letters because so few of them differentiate between their "bread and butter" and their "one-shots." Many salesmen, at all levels, are victimized by using commodity techniques for specialties and vice versa. This also applies to educators, ministers and lawyers. And it is the Achilles heel of staff communicators in larger retail establishments and in industrial companies. Even some blue chip companies are guilty of using commodity techniques for specialties.

EVALUATE YOUR SPECIAL MARKET NEED

This trap of "which golf club to use?" faces letter writers much more than it does writers of TV commercials, promotional materials, political speeches or newspaper advertising. For all starting writers of business letters, the first basic decision is embodied in the "specialty vs. commodity" propositions. While a correct evaluation of the marketing need is vital, it is not highly complex if considered directly in relationship to your business, position or profession.

Letter writing is the only economics related communications activity having more amateur or avocational practitioners than professional or vocational. Newspaper want ads are similar, but their total investment is peanuts compared to letters.

While there is no conflict, nor clear line of distinction, between occasional business letter writers and those writing them as part of their job, our discussions will be counterpoint as we approach letter elements. We shall not short-shrift the rhetoric and techniques of letter construction, but the guts of letter writing decisions is the product or service as it relates to the market. For example, a consumer item product (brand) manager or marketing services head for a large producer sets up a family of communications for new models. They include dealer meetings, field junkets, press meetings, trade magazine and consumer advertising schedules and a dozen more essentials. Obscure, but vital in these programs, are some items called "collateral." These are the little bridges and byways explaining strategy, dramatizing differences, instructing distributors and aids to dealers. They may even include the "introduction deal." This is where a letter to the big dealers, president to president, or a letter to chain marketing directors from their counterparts may make the difference. Or, when the new product is ready to go, a letter goes to all suppliers, financial interests, labor unions, each from his counterpart, keeping him interested. This is an example of the one-shot business letter whose function ends immediately, but whose effect may be felt for years.

PLANNING RULES FOR BUSINESS LETTERS

The standard planning rule for business letters is that they must be in sequences aimed at cumulative effect. That is the big end of both consumer and commercial letters for selling. The fact that three, six or a dozen letters, month after month, may be needed before the slightest impact is felt has no bearing on planned use of a "one-shot" that might bring the company its biggest day or month.

We hope this discussion of business letters as successfuly used by department stores, industries, gasoline or tire dealers and appliance stores will clarify the central fact about letters for selling: they must be planned to suit the offering, and they must be aimed at a visible market. Beginning writers should consider one-shot letters as technique polishers, but they are forewarned not to send a single letter where a series belongs and not to spend their money until they can see the market—or at least until they are strongly suspicious that there is life out there in the darkness.

PRE-WRITING MAKE-READY FOR A SINGLETON— A ONE-SHOT

Tentatively select your product or service and your market.

Analyze the product's acceptance, its use-characteristics, its availability in the marketplace, *its price-image*.

Select a list, or analyze carefully any customer list to determine, name by name, how they qualify as prospects. Example: a department store might elect furniture restoring; its names would come from older, upper middle-class homes. Or you may have a specialty as your stock in trade, such as carpeting for the home, low premium insurance, books, newer appliances or electric house wares, outdoor aids or shrubbery, low-acceptance office items such as refrigerators, or a health device. Non-book stores use books as specialties as do mail book sellers for their first sale.

TIMING: THE ONE-SHOT'S BIGGEST HAZARD

The single-purpose letter has as its greatest hazard the uncertainties involving split-second timing. Unless it is a seasonal repeat from other years, judging sales potentials of one-shots is largely guesswork except among the expert mail developers. A novel jewelry item that misfires slightly in December is really dead in January. There are some exceptions where reversing the seasonal demand creates a new market. Christmas greeting cards have a terrific January "close-out" demand. Similarly, obsolete electric housewares are at the big volume end for some producers.

In determining the item for a single letter, the key question is: "How many people would like it free?" Then ask "How many have one now?" If there is any doubt about basic acceptance, look for another item. Your item must be one that is wanted, but not needed.

Everybody puts his needs ahead of his wants. The answer to our second question is equally important. Very few items are specialties, or can be profitably sold by mail. Specialty selling does not work on commodities such as steam irons, vacuum cleaners or typewriters.

That is our background. It need hardly be suggested that you avail yourself of any possible list of known buyers, or of known users by need, such as air pilots, sales executives, etc. You know, or will learn quickly, that America is made up of individuals with established tastes and desires. For a baseball team to attract a million attendance during a season only a hundred thousand customers are needed. To sell a million books annually, the repeat factor is similar in type.

THE JOB OF ONE-SHOT LETTERS IS TO GET THE ORDER

To discuss the rhetoric of our letter we shall start at its close. On one-shot letters you must close them or kill them. Even some fairly sophisticated letter selling specialists are occasionally guilty of creating an interest, then not closing the sale. You must get a reply.

As pointed out earlier, letters are more a technique than a talent. In composing a one-shot letter your margin for error is zero. So you must make an outline which includes your objective and the make-up of your list. Known users? Occupational item? Economic qualification? Own similar products? Does your proposition relate to an established image price?

The typical good business letter should open a door for a salesman, but the real aim of the one-shot letter is to get an order in the mail. Let us try an example. Here we are using a list purchased from a travel agency listing:

> Dear Mr. Smith:
>
> We have developed an extended coverage travel and at-work health and accident policy that we are offering as a test-market estate plan directly to selected risks prior to offering through agents, that will cover you the moment the enclosed card, accompanied by 50 cents in coin, reaches our office.
>
> For that 50 cents you will be covered, under the terms of the benefits shown on the enclosed schedule, for a full 30 days from its starting date.

Under this binder arrangement, our Old Line company assumes the full burden during the period when you will have the policy for analysis and evaluation. Should you decide to continue its protection, we will allow you the net rate involving no agency or sales fees. You will decide whether you wish to continue the insurance while you are covered as described. Only then do you remit the $19.45 balance for a full year's coverage.

This offer is limited to return cards postmarked not more than ten days after your receipt of this letter. This unusual offer is being made to families known to be better-than-average risks. We suggest that you return the card immediately to gain this trial coverage. The offer will not be repeated beyond the brief test-market period.

        Cordially yours,

The cumbersome first paragraph tells the story of the benefits. Omitted is any reference to the value of insurance. To avoid misunderstanding, the short second paragraph tells specifically what the purchaser gets for his 50 cents.

The body, or comprehensive argument of the letter is the third paragraph. It is larded with reference to "binder," "Old Line" company, avoiding agency commission and coverage while deciding. Regardless of the merit (or appeal) of a proposition after it is stated, it must be proved or substantiated with answers to anticipated questions.

In one-shot letters, the letter in the reader's hand must do the entire job. Equally important to the proposition's appeal is a club to get action now. Most letters with one-shot offers must find a buyer who wants the product or service. If he is more eager than that he probably owns several such policies. While there is a factor of "no intention of buying" in all responses to trial offers, the general stability of your list is your safeguard.

In one-shot letters a typical recipient is a name originating in a "similar purchase" or occupational grouping. That indicates that the prospect has a price image in his mind. For example, at one time the lowest price tape recorders listed at $195. When an importer found one of similar attributes to sell profitably at $79, his one-shot letter to executives cleaned out his supply quickly. By the time he replenished, the market was aware of the lower price. On the other hand, ordinary table model letter-copiers are sold under $500, but seldom below $395. When an importer found a model to offer (by mail) at $149 the response was disappointing. He failed to identify his product with units in the $400 to $500 price range.

In our aim to give easy-to-do guidance on business letter writing, we deliberately have jumped into somewhat sophisticated marketing stereotypes. Our objective is to forewarn letter writers that the essence of letters that sell is the value of the proposition and the writer's understanding of his market (or of a single reader's interest). Now we would like to re-phrase some of our suggestions, putting everyday definitions on single letter aims.

MEET YOUR OBJECTIVE: RELATE TO READER NEEDS AND HABITS

The single letter is seldom a true test of any proposition. When your proposition is to hinge upon a single letter, you should give great attention to your objective. Be sure it comes across in the opening statement. Also, you should be fully acquainted with your recipient's buying, or selecting, habits. Your offer must be strictly related to what the buyer expects to pay. An office requiring administrative services of an added employee is aware of the going rates for recent college grads. A college grad with five years or more experience should state his "starting salary." A non-college writer also should supply his salary needs in his first (only) letter.

In sending one letter, all is lost for you unless you achieve your objective. If you sell your proposition but fail in its close you have set it up for the next applicant.

Your offer must be closely related to the needs or habits of the recipient. This does not require placing yourself in the buyer's shoes. Rather, it means having evidence that he has bought your specialty. All letters should show an understanding of how the prospect's situation fits our offer. As with bowlers, travelers, salesmen and others with recreational or occupational needs, many products and services identify, or name the market. This is significant in determining your sales objective or burden. The bowler does not need selling on bowling, nor the traveller on accident insurance. Nor is the salesman unaware of the use of travel kits. In one-shot letters, a part of the effectiveness of your proposition is your assumption that the reader who wants your product does so because he's in his job and successful. It should reflect that he must be interested because "everybody" is. Here is a parallel situation. You ask a man if he has a color TV set. "What make is it?" He doesn't answer that he hasn't a set. He more likely says, "Funny you ask me that. I went to a dealer and I said to him. . . ." Twenty minutes later you know he does not have color TV.

COMPANY-TO-COMPANY SINGLETONS

The one-shot commercial letter—company to company—is often only remotely related to the consumer specialty letter. They do have in common a single burden—it is seldom to build the business—and each has one chance to accomplish its mission.

Included in our in-context approach for letter writing, we shall discuss finding opportunities for letters. The commercial letter as a one-shot is most commonly used by industrials, and consumer manufacturers to dealers to open doors or make appointment overtures for their field man, distributors or agents. Not too uncommon, but effective, is the "I expect to be in your neighborhood . . ." from an industrial salesman to a buyer acquaintance. Also, not used nearly enough is the power of the letterhead when a sales manager writes to a prospect-executive introducing his suppliers' or his own field representative, even though the two executives are absolute strangers. These bread and butter door-openers make an almost magical contribution to marketing channels. But when a marketing director confines his "new program" coverage to such working materials, he is showing one difference between the work-a-day executive and the resourceful one. Such situations offer a fine chance for a president-to-president letter: "A view from the mountain top into and beyond the lush valleys where new products grow and blossom . . . and profits. . . ."

ONE-SHOT OPPORTUNITIES IN INDUSTRY
AND RETAILING

The one-shot letter in industry is suited to a new process, a new line of products or a new model. In retailing it may be to get sales for a specialty in established stores, or for merchandisers who know products short of acceptance with good "want factors" and clear price image identity as a bargain. For the politician, educator or other prestige citizen, it makes an effective vehicle for a show of friendship and "to share some information before it appears in the press." Our reference here is to a letter unaccompanied by "literature."

AVOID ENCLOSURES

Professional mailers usually know what value letters enclosed with flashy literature have. Their apparent uncertainty stems from the reader differences from one product list to another. Book buyer lists are made up of citizens who read labels on catsup bottles. You can't hide a letter from them no matter how you cover it with brochures. They avidly read the four-page book publisher's letter, printed from salutation to the president's signature cut.

To adhere to our statement that effective business letters are the application of a technique to a well understood selling situation, let us evaluate embellishments (enclosures) that affect the letter itself.

USING THE ONE-SHOT IN A SPECIAL RETAIL SITUATION

You are a partner in an appliance business that has just arranged to stock 100 electric dehumidifiers purchased at $25 each. They are Superba brand, but the company is dropping this production. You know, and many families know, that electric dehumidifiers have a fairly well fixed price image, between $70 and $90. The distributor agreed not to sell other stores at the $25 price, if you would advertise to move them at once. This is a good situation for a one-shot specialty letter. The dehumidifier has fallen short of commodity acceptance for 30 years. Your letter:

> Dear Mrs. Jackson:
>
> We have arranged, through a special purchase agreement with Superba company, to offer the new model automatic electric Superba Dehumidifier at a special price of $69.50. A leader among electric room dehumidifiers, we have represented and sold this product for

many years, at prices ranging from $84.50 to $89.50. By taking the entire stock of a warehouse oversupply, we have saved more than $25 on each unit, and we are passing a share of that saving on to our good customers.

The Superba unit absorbs from 9 to 16 gallons of moisture from the air in your home every 24 hours during the humid periods of the year. It is absolutely guaranteed for uninterrupted performance. Also, it has a moisture removal capacity not exceeded by any unit on the market, regardless of price.

I might mention that I have had a Superba Dehumidifier unit in my home for six years. It is hooked up to drain the water through a copper tube directly to the sewer. It has never failed nor required repair. It has made life greatly more pleasant during humid periods. Since our supply is limited, I would suggest that if you would like one of these you call me at the store very soon and I will earmark one for holding until you can get in to the store.

Very cordially yours,

A glance shows that the letter sums up the proposition in its opening. Its body identifies the product clearly with dehumidifiers in the $89.50 bracket. At the end it asks for the order. Many appliance dealers insist that such a letter should at least carry enough other product literature to use up the postage.

The one-shot specialty letter above is meant to do one job. If, when it is opened, out come some coupons, double stamps, and "10¢ off on light bulbs," the householder will put the coupons in her purse and never read the letter. Some industrial writers compose excellent letters, but when enclosed with such bread and butter items as specification sheets the letters are ignored.

ECONOMICAL ASPECTS OF SINGLE SPECIALTY LETTERS

Probably the most frequent negative quality in letters from retailers is their poor appearance. A good letter, processed with addressee's name typed in at the top, costs a minimum of 25 cents for composition and postage. An average mailing into a segment of suburban or medium-size city homes might be 250 names. At 25 cents each, the out-of-pocket would be $62.50 plus staff costs. To spend that money, for an appliance, furniture or wearable goods dealer, would require bringing in several sales. If the letter is planned as a one-shot for a specialty, that should not be over-burdening if the item is in the $20 or up class.

When retailers induce a shopper to ask for an item described in a letter, they have an opportunity to sell other items on the same trip. A note of caution is: always show the advertised product, with full endorsement, before any other product is mentioned.

CHAPTER IV

HOW TO ESTIMATE THE VALUE OF YOUR PROPOSITION IN PLANNING LETTERS TO CUSTOMERS AND STRANGERS

Letter writing's basic yardstick, the value of the proposition, measures all business letters alike: personal business, commercial or consumer. While the writer's skills may vary greatly, the occasional writer does not mis-evaluate his proposition any oftener than paid writers. Both appear to see their own proposition as if it should interest everyone. At least interest everyone on their list. Completely missing the target is the unfortunate experience of occasional writers such as elected club or civic officers more than of advertising or marketing executives who have considerable familiarity with products and customers. And non-paid writers seldom plan letter-series.

PLANNING PERSONAL BUSINESS LETTERS

To some degree, everyone can be a letter writer for his personal affairs or in his office seeking business. It may be an understatement to say that our nation has too much junk mail: Too much "Dear Occupant." We are on the side of the angels. We not only assume that all letters of the type we discuss are addressed to an individual, we also suggest first class mail. The vast majority of professional and business executives will never have occasion to use a consumer or commercial mailing, or even a letter-series, but practically everyone writes some business letters. All of these have three parts: 1) proposition; 2) justification; 3) conclusion. In following our outlines and suggestions, the elements of one writer's proposition often are identifiable with another's. Personal business letters invariably are planned to accomplish a mission. Their planning technique involves what to omit as well as what must be included.

YOUR PROPOSITION CARRIES IMPACT THROUGH MOTIVATION

In letters from companies or institutions the proposition must indicate awareness of other communications, letters or other. For example, a college administrator may occasionally write to alumni or others on various subjects, but if he writes for the "appeal" it's something else, unless it is a part of the development program. The right name may be an influential alumnus or citizen with economic pressure for the campaign proposition. All letter propositions must have the strongest element and the strongest signer.

In identifying elements for the proposition it should be borne in mind that the receiver should supply part of the motivation. Example: the letter to the newcomer. But here the writer must have a strong offer to get action—as all one-shot letters must have.

Big stores, in most communities the "name store," seldom neglect their customers' letters to the president. But the president rarely sees, or personally answers, many complaint letters.

DEPARTMENT STORE MAILING PROGRAMS

As the community's broadest user of advertising (chains and discount stores frequently out-hit them in the newspapers) many old line department stores have as many as three mailing programs simultaneously. These are repeated one-shot letters with no long-range plan, often enclosing a single folder offering full range of colors, or perhaps a special price. The second type is a series of letters planned to impress the customer with the store's prestige position, such as restaurants with unusual menus and parking convenience; exotic wares from far-off places; advance showings of style or fashion lines, etc. Very often these projects are nursed along by the top management. The other common type involving mailings is the monthly bill enclosure.

In our 55-store survey, one segment of 19 smaller stores representing housewares, appliances, hardware, liquor, laundry services and auto services, a surprising 14 enclosed one or more factory supplied folders with monthly bills. Only two of these had sent any letters with product folder enclosures. All said they had used factory postcards at one time or another. While fewer than half of these stores said they had, or could get mailing lists, many said, "Lists are no problem. Our own customers are the best list in town."

MANAGEMENT POLICY LETTERS—SHORT CUT TO STIMULATING DEALER INTEREST

The question asked these dealers regarding the availability of factory mailing literature brought a wide variety of answers. Many said that one or more distributors had offered mailing materials. A few said, "Factory material doesn't work in this town." Asked if the factory officials ever wrote to them, one answered that all big manufacturers' "top management" wrote to him. Most of them guessed they received some direct mail from manufacturers whose lines they carry. Conclusion: most larger manufacturers who occasionally send "policy" letters to dealers are not making much impact.

One appliance dealer with factory field organization experience was very aware that the president of his former employer had written him. "I was with them seven years and that's the only letter from him I ever saw," he said. The letter was part of a new model introduction plan. "I got a kick out of it," he said.

The consensus of a dozen calls on manufacturers' product managers was that these top brass letters may help, but some said they were written by writers with only sketchy knowledge of the president's role in marketing. It appears that present top management communications with dealers is in a low key. In turn, most dealers have little or no confidence in letters to their customers.

Casual talks with factory staff writers brought such comments as, "Whenever I've written something for the Old Man, it gets changed so I wouldn't recognize it." Several said, "We put it into our package. If it is used up front, they change it around. It's not a big thing." The conclusion is that factory managements seldom set up real objectives for this type of participation in marketing. Because dealers of all sizes apparently respect the top management of their manufacturers, these policy letters can effectively create dealer-interest by demonstrating an interest in the dealer's problems.

Suppose we are manufacturing power mowers. Our records show that not more than ten percent of our dealers stock our full line, and not more than half of them ever displayed more than six of our 12 models. Also three of our models show an aggregated factor of only six percent of our volume, even though they were subjects of special field and distributor incentive activities. The objective of our letter could be to try again to get a higher factor of early season model representation. Our new line should drop the slow movers. That decision was made in planning the new line. This gives us a worthwhile letter objective on policy. We have shortened the line to concentrate on faster moving models.

Proposition:

Dear Mr. Jones:

Following the greatest year in our history, Superba has shortened its line to increase dealer efficiency in displaying all models by eliminating the three slower moving numbers. Our studies show that nine of last year's 12 Superba mowers accounted for almost 95 percent of its sales, and the dealers getting the higher volumes invariably showed sales in all of these nine classes. You will take no risk in ordering the full line. You may return for full credit any units not sold from your stock order after 30 days. We want every unit on your floor to be in demand at all times.

This proposition is rather lengthy, but when writing regarding a situation where the reader is making a financial commitment, he will read carefully—he wants the whole story. Since well established brand manufacturers do not normally tell dealers (it's the distributor's area) that they will take back unsold models, it is worth including that as part of the proposition.

THE VITAL FACTOR: RESPECT YOUR
READER'S PRE-KNOWLEDGE

"Return unsold units" appears to be stronger than "shortened line." However, it is estimated that many dealers would doubt good faith if asked to stock units known to be slow. So we should first tell them we have corrected our line.

In letters to familiar customers (dealers or consumers) if the proposition adheres to genuine issues regarding products or policies, the burden of the letter's body is greatly reduced. In the above proposition the dealer's obvious lack of interest in the slow selling models is recognized by a new policy that supports his judgment. The offer to take back unsold units justifies his stocking all models.

As we shall discuss later, a great many commercial letters fail because the writer does not understand the reader's pre-knowledge. In effect many letters say "Tomorrow the sun will rise," when they perhaps should say "Tomorrow, when the sun rises . . . ." In our business world with its standardized equipment, methods and sources of information, the air is saturated with information, and most of it is well established. When a reader picks up a letter telling him something a child should know, he immediately tosses the letter into the wastebasket. No one will stand still while a volunteer advisor tells him how to run his business. Broadening our reference point, the rule of accurate estimates on readers' present knowledge related to our proposition is a vital factor in composing letters that are read clear to the end.

ESTABLISHING STRONG READER APPEAL IN CONSUMER LETTERS

In reading dozens of consumer letters signed by presidents or other top officers it was observed that a majority showed no respect for any possible reader pre-knowledge of the respective products. Most of these specimens over-proved their propositions by stating a series of advantages instead of establishing one benefit. Almost without exception the letters were accompanied by enclosures with items such as redemption coupons, money-back offers and free offers. Their propositions were generally obscured by exclamatory headlines: "Now!! New!! Sensational Savings!!! Read!!!" In our switching from consumer to commercial examples our intent is to show that letters are a formula of communications that brings returns proportionate to the effort and skill put into them. The true value of any proposition must await returns; but we can show elements that are present in winners, and in losers.

OMIT THE OBVIOUS IN COMPANY-TO-COMPANY LETTERS

In top management company-to-company letters the writer should gamble on omitting all obvious benefits that the reader may already know. It takes only one advantage, and it may not represent a world-shaking benefit, to influence a favorable decision. An industrial letter that says ". . . will eliminate one operation . . ." may have far greater strength than broad claims to double profits.

In setting up your proposition its scope, or range of matters involved, is your first consideration. That will take care of the pre-knowledge question. As a TV dealer your proposition should not "sell" solid state. It should not sell color either. Both of these are in the pre-knowledge realm. Similarly you would not sell credit, out of the high rent district or money-back if not satisfied. The one perennial left to TV dealers is service. All retailers always have savings.

EFFECTIVE ELEMENTS IN MANAGEMENT POLICY LETTERS

Now let us return to the Superba power mower president's letter to dealers. On his proposition we added "We want every unit on your floor to be in demand at all times." That idea represents dealers' dreams. In the relationship of dealers to the brands they represent there is considerable emotion. If Superba is a specific dealer's top line in price and volume, he is gratified to learn its line is more realistic. His gratification is enhanced at hearing directly from Superba's president. This element may be diluted as he reflects that every dealer is getting this letter. So, our justification should strongly indicate that he is not "just another dealer." (If he has no special value to Superba nothing is lost by our indicating that he has.) Top management letters should omit non-performing dealers.

Body: (Justification)

I am taking the liberty of writing to some of our best dealers regarding the new policy of concentrating only on the faster selling models before it is announced in our trade advertising and publicity. Later, we shall release figures that clearly point to a 20 percent gain in power mower purchases in the coming season. We share with you the responsibility of earning our full share of that increase. To assure ourselves and dealers that we are planning for this, our present production schedules call for an increase of 20 percent plus the five percent lost on the discontinued models. My only word of caution to our dealers is this: the most popular and best selling models are most likely to be in short supply temporarily as the season advances. You may have as your guide your last year's experience. Please protect yourself on the faster movers.

If the proposition has appeal, the supporting facts must justify ordering the full line. While neither the proposition nor body shown above is edited for final drafts, the absence of strong selling points is deliberate. Dealers buy as a way to profit. On favored lines they want strong displays, but not models that don't move. The handsome letter on engraved stationary bearing the president's signature has impressed him. But he must reconcile possibly over-ordering. His justification is the reminder that the most popular models are in shorter supply than others at season's peak.

INTRODUCING NEW MODELS TO DEALERS AND CUSTOMERS

The strength of top executive letters to do a working job can be shown where established brands are showing a new line. The objective of letters accompanying first dealer showings often is to broaden brand acceptance within the dealer organization. Most competing manufacturers bring out their new lines at approximately the same time and a top management letter may be the competitive difference.

If a dealer is influenced to stock or increase his inventory of a line through a letter, maybe he can get his season underway with a similar letter to his customers, using the same proposition.

As in recent seasons, we shall feature Superba Power Mowers this season and are now planning a private showing of the new models. You are invited to come in between 6:30 and 9:00 any evening next week, from Monday through Friday evenings when the store is not open for business. Enclosed is your admittance card with our number, HE 2-5603. Just let us know when it is convenient for you to come in on any Tuesday, Wednesday or Friday evening.

The idea of that proposition is to set apart Superba from the many new lines being introduced. Evening showings are not always productive of sales, but most families receiving such an invitation will be aware of the store and brand if the letter is properly handled in planning.

A RELIABLE RETAIL IMAGE ENDORSES PERSONAL SELL LETTERS

The first paragraph is your proposition in most straight selling or door opening letters, but it is inseparable from the writer's name and the recipient's name. A good proposition must come from the right person, and good propositions must reach the families with the potential to buy—its market—with the desire to acquire the product once they know about it, or to have the service offered.

For a dealer's power mower offer we must have a home owner; probably one who is a present user of a power mower that is ready for replacement. At the letter's end the signer's name should mean integrity to householders of the neighborhood. A dealer often has the image of soundness and reliability to a greater extent than he realizes. An advantage of a letter-offer over less personal advertisements is that it offers a chance to say, "We stand behind our products, beyond the warranty of the manufacturer. The best mower service in the city." Where a retail store has a large following because of the reputation of its owner or head man, he should sign the letter. His signature means: "I personally endorse this offer as the best we have ever made on a mower."

PROPOSITIONS FOR IMMEDIATE OR LONG TERM ACTION

Suppliers of personal and home services such as insurance, real estate, burial facilities and landscaping are among the more sophisticated personal business letter users. At the other extreme, conventional retailers in stores (except big stores) very seldom write personal business letters for five hundred or a thousand neighbors or customers. Their commonest reason is, "It just takes too much time and it's not cheap." Yet the semi-professional services category knows it must seek out buyers, go to their homes or offices, while the smaller store people wait for customers to come in.

Innumerable informal survey-calls have established that neither of these categories often sit down and noodle out a good proposition to put into a letter. For services, the proposition that stirs a latent want is usually more effective than a proposition that might bring in an immediate order or two over the phone. When shooting for an immediate order, the proposition should be ". . . a seasonal shipment now being put on display. While we still have a full choice, we would like to invite you to come in and let our specialists specify the size and type suited to your lawn. Or, if you will mark the enclosed card and drop it in the mail, he will stop and inspect the conditions at your home dictating the mower equipment best suited. . . ."

RETAIL, COMMERCIAL AND CIVIC PERSONAL BUSINESS LETTER PROPOSITIONS

In citing propositions for various retail personal business letters we usually assume that companies are known to consumers. In commercial letters we assume that the two companies at least know of each other. For civic personal letters we assume that the signature is used because it has power. The signature might be that of a public figure in banking, education, industry or public life. For all of these types, that name becomes a part of the proposition.

Officers and staff of semi-public civic organizations or funds sending out personal business letters should familiarize themselves with the techniques industrial suppliers use among themselves. Often the head of a large supply company is better known in industry than are the top officers of his customers' companies. In that world where the communications cross-fire of big money selling offers fills the air, the trick is to get a message to the decision-maker. The top man can send a letter to his counterpart and get attention, but it is not easy to transfer this magic to get orders once the representative goes over the buyer's head. These suppliers meet this situation daily. Feelings are bruised, but when sales can't be made one way, they always try another. The proposition that gets action depends upon the top official's signature.

"INSIDE INFORMATION" LETTERS TO DEALERS AND CUSTOMERS

Where the president of any company—retail, manufacturer or service group—is well-known and influential, his letterhead is itself a vehicle for sales letters. For example, a well-known head of an appliance manufacturer might sign letters to four levels when a new product program is launched. These would be: 1) his own field organization; 2) distributor principals; 3) corporate heads of customer companies and 4) strategic non-customer company heads. When letters from a well-known man say ". . . am writing before this goes to the newspapers . . ." many of those getting it will show it around. When a well known industrialist gives advance information, it is common for his own representative to hear that the customer received advance information "from your president."

The relatively familiar gambit of "before it is announced" will not be too effective with stranger companies. The implication of inside information has value only in customer letters. The executive who would throw a stranger letter into the wastebasket with its offer of "pre-sale bargains" may be favorably impressed when he receives such a letter from a regular supplier. Magazines and book publishers find that a very successful technique for the mailing lists that they trade back and forth is to call everyone an "old customer." The value of letting customers be the "first to know" is a matter of their pride. Sales representatives in industries frequently give advance notice of a year or two when "coming out with a new machine."

CHAPTER V

FURTHER NOTES ON ESTIMATING THE VALUE OF YOUR PROPOSITION IN PLANNING LETTERS TO CUSTOMERS AND STRANGERS

In writing to stranger companies, care must be taken to avoid assuming that the recipient knows as much about your field as you do.

Before we examine some specific openings for letters to noncustomers and those who do not know us, let us take a look at what may be the most self-destroying opening gambit. This is the sentence that starts:

"As everyone in the tool industry is aware. . . ." No matter what you say, if it is about yourself you have lost a reader. If he continues after that opening his motive is curiosity. First, never assume that a stranger knows any specific thing. If he knows it, that is perhaps to the good; if he doesn't know it, or believe it, you have put yourself into the position of shaming him. Many highly successful salesmen gain concessions by looking prospects in the eye and telling them "Everybody in the industry knows. . . ." That may work when you are present, but never put it in a letter.

A second version of this over-stated method of assumption is the rhetorical question: "How would you like to have a new machine that does the work of six men and pays for itself in six months?" Even with the flood of publicity on electronic appliances no one believes a stranger is going to offer such a machine by mail. For letters going to your own industry, your only hope in going to heads of unfamiliar companies is that it opens the door. Even more to the point: do not open a letter to a busy man with a question.

PLANNING NEW PRODUCT OR NEW SERVICE LETTERS

In many industries a producer or supplier may be widely known in one area and practically unknown in another. In planning a letter to announce a new product or service which offers an opportunity that should not be overlooked, select your audience with the same care that you devote to your proposition. It may be that your first move should be to select a geographic area. If you adopt that method, examine the mailing list first. This gives you the opportunity to remove the names of present or recent customers.

LARGER TO SMALLER COMPANY LETTERS

The method of opening a letter from a large company to an unacquainted company and one from a small company may differ considerably. If yours is a widely known name, such as Western Electric, you do not tell them who you are. On the other hand, this widely known affiliate of the largest American company has many products and services whose applications are sometimes unknown even to those in related industries. An executive letter from Western Electric will have no difficulty reaching the top level after arrival. But its path from there on can be far less certain. Suppose it is addressed to neighbor companies in a plant city aimed at improving opinion that may have an effect on employee morale. Because most recipients would have very different employee problems, and there is invariably some competitive factor among companies as employers, its first hazard would be lack of sympathy in smaller companies with the problems of larger companies. Under such circumstances your first consideration should be an opening that would establish a common ground. Writing to a small foundry you would avoid ". . . us fellow employers out here in Plant City. . . ."

The foundry operator would scoff at that: he usually blames the large companies for negative community conditions. Your approach should be:

> In our continuing efforts to be a good neighbor here in Plant City, we sometimes observe negative situations developing sooner than

some because of our size being great. During the past year there has been sizeable unemployment that is of concern to all of us.

This opening is supplied to indicate some of the elements that should be considered by large companies writing to smaller ones. First: "our efforts . . ." has the unassuming tone that sets well with the smaller operator. Next, we say, ". . . sometimes . . ." to avoid the absolute connected with large company operations, and we clear the air by mentioning that we are a larger company.

The same elements are present in marketing letters from larger to smaller companies. Smaller company executives very often are sensitive regarding comparisons or relationships with giants. That sensitivity usually stems from social or other relationships; but it may have roots in negative attitudes from past experience. Upon reflection, executives of large companies are aware of differences between their companies' policies and those of small outfits. The time to pause and estimate the viewpoint of a smaller company executive is before you approach him in a letter.

SMALL COMPANY EXECUTIVES WRITING LARGE COMPANY EXECUTIVES

If there is some basic truth in these emotional factors when a large company approaches a smaller one, it is not nearly so basic, nor so negative to establishing a relationship as when the approach is reversed, from small company to the larger one. Small companies frequently say of larger ones, "Their problems have nothing in common with ours." Larger company executives invariably think that without bothering to express it.

When a letter from an unknown small company arrives at the office of a top executive of a larger company, according to procedure it is routed to a department head, with a pre-formed letter going to the sender telling him the recipient's name. In some larger companies the department head notifies the sender that he has the letter. Neither of these is purely negative although if your proposition requires the attention of the top man you missed your target.

PRESIDENT-TO-PRESIDENT LETTERS TO INTRODUCE "UNKNOWNS"

Experience has taught executives in large companies that very few otherwise unknown product or service offerings are worth pursuing. This reluctance to investigate may be caused by their own tight schedules. Also, their attitude may be that if any proposition is worthwhile they already know about it. In that sense the smaller company executive has a more formidable task in breaking through. Whichever way the flow is, our need is to be aware of the reversing of viewpoints. In large commercial mailings the names should be separated into "large" and "small" companies. Those going to the larger ones (with no record of previous dealings with smaller company sender) would start:

> Normally we do not have occasion to approach larger companies with whom we have not been doing business. However, at the behest of one of our larger customers we have developed a tape-control machine tool that attaches threaded fasteners without requiring a special operation, thus eliminating an operation without disturbing the present fabrications method.
>
> In recent months we have delivered three units of this tool to its original user, and have decided to make it available to stamping fabricators and others large enough to require a tool of its capacities. We would like to arrange for a working demonstration through your design engineers. . . ."

The words ". . . eliminating an operation . . ." are the key words that justify this as a president-to-president letter. Also, its sketchy description of function (in feeling out market potentials for new methods, developers seldom disclose details) there is little here that would excite purchasing agents, design engineers or others who see numerous tools whose costs eat up possible savings. Presidents make day-to-day work out of savings; often all he need do is scribble on your letter "let's take a look at this" and a staffer will be on the phone with you to arrange a showing.

In introducing any newer method, smaller companies approaching the big companies find the going slow after they show it to the purchasing people. Normally engineers (who would be the next step) have numerous cost-reduction operations in process. To presidents and general managers cost reductions are more abstract than to engineers, they look for savings everywhere.

The first sentence sets apart the letter from others written by unknowns by explaining you are not known to him. A top officer will not stop reading there. Your next sentence goes directly to work. An offer of a newly designed machine tool to reduce a cost ". . . for companies your size. . . ."

Were we writing from a large well-known company to a smaller outfit with whom we have had no past dealings, we have the same obligation to explain our letter. That is the entry to our full statement of the proposition. For example:

> This division of our company develops machine tools and other automated equipment for short and moderate production runs. We have recently proved-in a tape-control press especially designed for short-run operations. Its moderate initial cost in view of its cost reduction potentials has created a considerable interest among production engineers in companies with characteristic runs of this type.

Industrial sales are made through well-established and well-known channels within customer companies. In the long run all regular suppliers hew closely to the formula. It is only when a supplier's selling force is not reaching a company, or when their results are inadequate, that a top officer to top officer letter is sent. Sales representatives never write to top officers, unless they are also purchasers.

REASONS FOR WRITING

In both of the examples above, the opening sentence explains the reason for writing. You say or imply size of company as the essential element in your proposition. You explain that, and the reader knows you mean his company as he proceeds to read. The other sentence tells the top officer that your interest is in cost reduction. In all letters aimed at non-customer companies, it is doubly important that your opening tell your proposition, and that it is confined to that. Suppose your letter reaches the head of a recently modernized company with new tooling. He knows after one sentence whether it fits his company or not. If not, he is not irritated, very possibly he will acknowledge your letter and boast a little.

SIZING UP YOUR MARKET

In estimating the market for a piece of equipment, component or industrial product, you must always carefully evaluate its application or use-value in the operations of the prospect. The surest way to do this is to document its use, savings, profits and other characteristics in service of its present user. For example, should you have a product that is useful in the operations of one electric or gas utility company, it may be equally useful to other utilities. One difference common to utilities from other industrial companies is that utilities stand more unvaryingly on protocol. A letter to the president invariably is sent to the operating department, frequently after he or an assistant reads it. These operating people are doubly sure to carefully examine any proposition that comes from the office of the big boss.

When you are estimating the value of your proposition to a mailing list that appears proper for your product or service, the easiest method of proceeding is to divide the attributes of your proposal into three segments:

1. The product or service description (opening)
2. How and why it is for him (body)
3. How and when the next step comes (close).

PERSONALIZING LETTERS

All letters of the types we are discussing must be personally addressed and personalized otherwise where possible. That does not mean individually typed, but it does mean a printing job that looks as if it were typed singly, and the name must be filled in so as to appear a part of the typist's work. You should not mail a proposition to a company without knowing the nature of that company. Many companies are listed among manufacturers who do not literally operate facilities.

These include brands purchased for private labels. In most industries it is possible to learn which companies are prime producers and which buy components or products for their own labels. If your letters are going to the wrong companies, or to the wrong executives in any companies, you are not giving yourself a chance to get a fair return

WHEN TO DIRECT SALES PROPOSALS TO COMPANY BUYERS

While we have urged directing sales-proposal letters to the presidents of unfamiliar companies where representatives either do not call or do not make progress, there is no hard rule. For example, in situations where your field representative or jobber cannot or does not make the call, the first letter might be sent by your sales director to the purchasing agent. We have estimated that the president of any company we write to is very busy and receives piles of mail. That same is true of the purchasing agent. To make matters more difficult with the buying executive, his mail is full of proposals from established supply sources, companies well known to him with whom he has no current dealings, and confirming letters of matters already discussed.

Generally speaking, no letter that suggests a possible personal call should be sent before you know how and when the call is to be made. That is essential in writing to buyers. They commonly answer all mail proposals by sending a card telling when they see salesmen. Your only move then is to make the call. Should a letter to a buyer bring no answer, then the letter to the president should be sent with no mention that a letter was sent to the buyer. The first letter will have been from marketing, the second one from your president.

ANALYZING YOUR MAILING LIST

In evaluating your proposition's strength with the mailing list in front of you, you can determine how strong it may be by examining the companies who will get it. By the same token, you will be able to see how many of the companies are direct industry operating companies, as against holding companies at one extreme and divisions of complex corporations on the other. The general manager of corporate operating divisions is the equivalent of a president of a single unit operating company. For example, there is no way of estimating a proposition's value to the corporate head of DuPont, General Electric or General Foods. But the head of an operating division of a corporation of those types would not differ greatly from the president or executive vice president of an operating company.

LETTER BODY DESCRIBES YOUR PROPOSITION

The body of a proposition letter has the responsibility for acquainting the executive with *how*. That description should not be written by your engineering specialists. Yet, if it pertains to an engineering formula, it should be rewritten from the engineering specifications or other data. But its main function is to describe the process, qualities or applications. For example, if you have a product that appears suited to banks, your letter should convey what size or capacity bank it suits. Or if it is an expendable item, its shipping lots upon which prices are based must be clearly indicated. If yours is a specialty with status aspects your letter should assume—and indicate—the size institution best suited. As are many businesses, banks may be local chains with 100 offices, or single units doing neighborhood services. Very often their needs are unrelated. They are a prime example of the small business vs. big business debate. Smaller banks respond to offers with prices geared to their quantities; larger bank purchasers look for quantity discounts. In letter planning for all businesses, the size or volume factors should be among the first considerations in our objectives.

RE-CAST LETTERS TO MEET DIFFERENT
VOLUME FACTORS

According to apparent effects of size upon type of purchases, suppliers dealing with a wide range of small and large companies should experiment with re-casting letters by size of customer. That privilege is one of the letter's (and direct mail's) almost exclusive advantages.

Size of prospective buyers may create two or more markets within a single business category. Bankers, for example, often tell salesmen "That might work for the (big or little) fellow, but it wouldn't work for us."

Good propositions must look good for, and suited to, the reader at a glance. A bank president going through his mail may have an outer office filled with customers. He almost hopes he can toss out each letter after the first sentence. If you enclose a printed piece, he may glance at that before he notices your letter. This is happening in the morning when the pressure is greatest. In his hurry, if the product folder misfires he may by-pass or overlook the letter, letting it go into the wastebasket or sending it along to the purchasing agent.

YOUR LETTER CLOSE MOTIVATES ACTION

In suggesting that the body of the letter take the full responsibility for describing the product, we are aware that printed matter is available for that specific purpose. Our reason for not suggesting sending it and killing two birds with one stone is that it can easily supersede the letter. When we write in our letter body how the product can help him, the recipient must look further to learn what comes next. That is our close.

The close of a letter to a top executive may be to inform him that the sender has a new brochure, specification sheet or illustration that he would like to send along. It may be that a jobber, or representative in the territory, would like to call. Or it may be that we would like to hear more about his needs.

If your proposal seems to have merit for company heads, and it can be described to indicate its worthwhileness as something to be looked into, that leaves it up to our close to motivate action. Some letters that are very effective in doing the first two things fail at the end because they imply over-anxiety. When an executive discusses a matter with his counterpart in a supplier company they leave it on some informal basis such as, "I'll give you a call and bring our engineer around," or the supplier may say, "I'll tell our man to drop in at your purchasing department and mention your interest." No matter how urgent it is, the supplier rarely pressures his friend. There is a big difference between a weak close and a proper close.

APPRAISE YOUR FOLLOW-UP STEPS

The appraisal you make as to the best way to take the next step may be the most important decision involved in your letter. The most commonly sought answer is permission to have our man see your man. That leaves it that the president must tell you who our man should see. In one sense, it might seem that our man could go after the business without your letter if that "name of the buyer" is all that he gets. Actually the president of the company will not suggest that his buyer be visited unless he thinks your proposal has merit.

In situations where the product does not involve a regularly purchased item, the chief executive may suggest that your representative visit his chief engineer, sales head or personnel man. A good rule to follow on these is that very often those executives know that the president does not suggest seeing them unless a cost-cutting item or process is involved.

In the foregoing discussion we are assuming that there have never been any business dealings between the companies involved. That does not make the letter greatly different than if they were between companies well-known to each other. Where your letter goes to the head of a company you now do business with, its road is not nearly so rocky. Your opening should be, "As one of your suppliers of tools for production, I am writing to tell you of a new development before it is announced to the trade. . . ."

Among the types of letters that fail most frequently are those sent by one industrial company or engineering service to another industrial company or to a governmental body. This does not necessarily indicate a lack of business sense or skill. Rather, most technically skilled executives feel that facts are all that matter. Many of them have the weight of success on their side, but that success is seldom even remotely related to what they write. The nature of a business enterprise that is highly technical minimizes the need for a best foot forward with strangers.

SETTING UP YOUR LETTER—DEFINE YOUR PROPOSITION IN ONE SENTENCE

After placing an extremely high value on letter content as the prime element in its effectiveness, we place care in selecting addresses as second in importance. Once you have your total proposal materials ready and a list properly segregated by size of companies, companies to whom you are known and others, and special considerations made as to which executive should be approached first, you are ready to set up your letter. An easy method of working out your opening sentence is to try to define your total proposition in one sentence. For example: "A machine tool that performs four tasks formerly requiring four tools and capable of commensurate cost savings." It is not advisable to volunteer that a process or a machine cuts out men. If you have figures showing savings, do not put that reference into the opening. It may be effective in the close, but the opening is aimed at interesting the executive by highly ethical statements. Throwing dollar savings there is too high pressured.

CHAPTER VI

HOW TO GO ABOUT THE LETTER BODY

Justification—Credibility—Timing

When we have written a convincing and appealing proposition for the reader who picks up our letter, our next move will be to justify, to bring credibility. We must offer the supporting facts that will convince our reader that the proposition is a good one for him now.

Whether our letter is to a dealer offering a new profit line, to an industrial with a cost-saving new process, or to a civic-minded citizen for the annual campaign, it must justify action upon its mission. We have told him what we want. Now we give him the evidence to prove he should act favorably, preferably in his own interest.

The letter body invariably should support our proposition, but there is no widely practiced formula for all types of business letters. The job-seeking letter's body is your personal education and business profile; the manufacturer to dealer letter tells how and why you can bring him an added 10 percent profit; the letter on giving explains why and how this year's need is greater and the commercial-industrial letter cuts a cost, it says, and the body discloses a credible new technique.

RHETORICAL QUESTIONS LOSE READERS

There are many ways of effectively telling a story to sell, but even more ways of losing a reader. The commonest way to lose him enroute after he has started to read the body is to ask him a rhetorical question. That is not the only way, but it is the most frequent. Asking questions, hoping to let a reader corner himself, seems to be a compulsion with some writers. That may be good technique in speeches, in feature stories and perhaps in consumer selling, but in a business letter it is out of place. In commercial letters rhetorical questions are very rarely permissible.

JUSTIFYING YOUR PROPOSITION: STRENGTH IN RESTRAINT

When writing letters many good personal salesmen weaken their position by exaggerations unnoticed in speaking. Terms such as "revolutionary," "sensational," and "astounding" are seldom effective as helps to proof. Strong statements are necessary, but strength is best shown through restraint. While some unrestrained writing is caused by the urge to get across the points, generally the unconvincing body of a business letter results from lack of a clearly thought-through objective.

In our opening statements telling what we want, we have struck a nerve if the reader continues on into the letter body. He may hope that your promise is justified. Then he reads of a "revolutionary design to bring million dollar profits." Even a hint of such intemperate claims loses executives in the larger companies, and smaller business men are skeptical about "big profits."

FINDING YOUR STRONGEST JUSTIFICATION

The easiest way to evaluate your proposition and to determine its strongest justification is to list your points before you start writing. First, the objective then, numerically, the facts that support it. For example:

Letter objective:
to sell a newly developed home broiler-roaster.
Proposition:
To dealers 50 percent profit on unit using 120V electric current, at $39.95 list; or 25 percent profit when discounted for selling at

$29.95. Full warranty for one year; unsold goods returnable by dealer any time within 90 days.

Body:
1. Send letter in early November for Christmas
2. Buy direct from factory: price for 3-piece orders
3. Modern factory gives us low costs
4. Specialized broilers gaining acceptance
5. Strong gift item
6. Strong "leader" for discount advertising
7. Product leaflets (enclosed) at $15 per 1,500

The seven points listed above may not include the best reasons for a dealer to stock an "unknown," but the specialty nature of the item offered means that most of his regular suppliers seldom push them with basic electric housewares for the Christmas gift season. Among the first decisions in letter planning is the timing. In consumer goods sales planning the item should be defined as for "use" or "gift." In dealer letters it is sufficient to say what a product does, and its warranty period. Confine the major proof to reasons it is profitable to sell. In consumer items through the mail there must be a savings. While we urge that business letters do their own selling job, when they are related to specific products a letter-size product or line folder should be clipped to the letter.

SUBSTANTIATING THE PROPOSITION

All letter bodies have in common that they should substantiate the proposition. We should strive for fresh, clear ways of telling dry facts, but it is better to have a letter body plodding than flippant. It must cover the specifics that are questions in the reader's mind. Letters to dealers on processed stationery that omits commercial advertising are usually read by dealers themselves or by their decision-making managers. The industrial letter has a rougher time getting to the head man.

Letters to larger industrial companies selling such products as tools and components often are routed to department heads rather than to the addressed man in the head office. If they look like "prestige" they pass into the inner sanctum. Then the proposition must have interest. Now we come to the body. It need not be brisk or appealing. If the executive is reading it, he is interested in the supporting evidence for your proposition. Your facts should be worked into context in the order of their importance.

HOW A SMALL COMPANY JUSTIFIED GIANT CORPORATION CONSIDERATION

In industrial selling, salesmen may be calling upon companies whose buyers deal with more than 5,000 suppliers. Each category of these sees a buying group or individual who represents such purchases as engineering decisions or production, some to purchase ready-made parts or tools, others to secure bids for specially engineered and produced components, tools or parts. Calling on larger accounts, the salesman may become known to two or three specialists, but he will be completely unknown at what is called the decision-making level.

This technical sounding situation has its counterpart in almost every form of retailing, in thousands of situations involved in giving to worthy causes, and in the selection of facilities for vacation, travel, entertainment and recreation. There is a chicken and egg circle in getting messages across. The big fellows get big because they have the funds to tell their stories, or they have the funds to tell their stories because they are big. The communications aspects of size must never be overlooked when writing a selling letter. You must use your size as a reason he needs you. Let us write to a big corporation from our small industrial fastener company saying that we will conduct a demonstration clinic of a new automated fastener that eliminates one handling operation. Now we are ready to justify consideration from the president of a billion-dollar corporation.

Body:
We have had considerable engineering cooperation from the automotive and aviation industries during development of this process. As you know, threaded fasteners are mandatory in many applications requiring detachability and vibration imperviousness. That we can install them as a part of existing operations impresses engineers. The corollary reason we would like you to see the installation process is that the process requires investment in a new machine tool. Budget-burdened engineers are properly hesitant. It is a tool that will pay its way many times over, but it does require an investment decision. . . .

The proposition on the above letter was a personal invitation to visit the supplier's engineering laboratory, at the reader's convenience during a three-day period, to see this automated machine in action.

The "close" may tell the demonstration hours, and a naive-sounding ". . . will look forward to seeing you. . . ." This letter was sent to the presidents of divisions, general managers and central staff officers of all of the Detroit automobile manufacturers. Within 24 hours the telephone started ringing. The presidents turned over the letters to staff assistants. They in turn started an inquiry, "Who has seen this? The big boss wants to know." Officers of Division general managers called. Five general managers visited (out of 17 car industry divisions then). During the three days 600 buyers, engineers, vice presidents, etc. visited the demonstration. Unbelievable? Yes, the fastener executives couldn't believe it. Why did they come?

The justification is the "investment in a tool." Out of 100 suppliers whose unit requires buying a special tool, 99 wait until the prospect is sold on the product before mentioning the tool. Buyers were impressed until the tool cost was mentioned. The letter practically told the top people, "Your buyers want this, but they are afraid to mention buying a machine tool." That letter was written five years ago. Today every automobile of a Detroit maker has more than 100 of these fasteners. The highest price cars have more than 200.

THE RULE IN WRITING STRANGER DECISION-MAKERS

There is a letter writing rule involved. It is this:

> When you write to a decision-maker as a stranger and tell him you have something that will save a lot of money for him he rarely believes you no matter how you say it. But if you tell him it will save a lot of money and eliminate an operation, unbelievable as that would be to a Detroit manufacturer, he believes you when you say, in effect: "The catch is, you invest in a tool."

CREDIBILITY COMES WITH THE "CATCH"

In offering unusually attractive rewards you must have a distraction-catch. Tools are not bought by buyers in big industries. Buyers shun solicitations involving tools unless stipulated. The top management knows all that. When they see ". . . process that cuts out an operation . . ." that is fine, but dubious. When they learn of tool investment they get the point. They wonder if their engineers have looked at the product.

The foregoing rule applies to all big offers. It is a version of "out of the high rent district," or "selling them for advertising purposes." Please bear in mind that the justification (not credibility) must be fully established. The credibility is eased when you mention the "catch." The catch should be an element that would cause most buyers and managers to lose interest, but not the manager we are addressing. It should be stated to whet his interest.

LETTER CONTENT, PROPERLY DIRECTED, IS WHAT SELLS

Bear in mind: the letter content is what sells. Nifty prose seldom helps a business letter sell, except books and other reading matter. In our example we used an obscure industrial type solicitation to establish that you should show awareness of what is good for the reader. Inferentially, that means your best mailing list is your own—one growing out of relationships. In all commercial letters the sharp difference between the right company and one not suited is vital. In industrial letters the right man in the right company is vital. Your letter must go where its logical entry is instantly recognized. Then it must tell your deal, and justify consideration.

Our example is president to president. Its central appeal is cost. That's almost a management word. When writing to engineers or purchasers remember they want product or service facts. Below the top officers supply facts—for maintenance, engineering, production or selling functions. That means specifications, data and perhaps a handsome brochure or folder. Buyers or functionaries with repeated uses for products or services have files on qualified suppliers. Your first objective is to get into the file.

TIMING MAILINGS FOR SALES SLOW-DOWNS OR PEAKS

Industrial suppliers encountering sales slow-downs often call in an agency and order a mailing. Often that mailing is motivated entirely by the sender's need, regardless of market conditions. Timing must be involved. Start your business-stirring letters from the customer's viewpoint. Are we pushing the wrong item? Are your products in over-supply? Very often a top officer should go see a few customers. He might learn something that would change his thinking. The opposite condition—when market supplies are short and your lines are hot—could well be the strategic moment to write a solicitation letter. When good companies offer early deliveries and slow deliveries are the order of the day, it leaves a fine and lasting impression.

Letters should be viewed in the commercial world as instruments of communications when business is either good or bad for the same reason. When sales are slow you want good orders from the best customers you can get. When business is brisk, you should take advantage of the time to upgrade your list of customers and broaden your base for new products or lines.

ALWAYS STRESS QUALITY

In letters you should always emphasize quality by telling something about the engineering, materials, design, volume or your company's experience in that field. Avoid such terms as "top quality" or other generalities. In the abstract, quality is now a catchword, one of those lazy man's words. If you ask 100 passers-by on the street which company makes the best quality cars they vote 60, 70 or 80 percent for the largest maker. That is true of all branded products. Why? If a guy likes a minority make, he still votes for the winner. That is true of all products. The term quality, in the personal sense used in letters or surveys belongs to the biggest. In commercial letters use costs, time-saving, eliminating an operation or anything where you aim at a nerve. Your proposition must strike a want, or an irritation point.

LETTERS TO OVERCOME NEGATIVE SITUATIONS

Let us suppose, each using his own example, that we are writing to our several markets with a proposition saying we can overcome a negative situation he has suffered for some time.

We might be an appliance manufacturer writing to a dealer suffering from cut-throat price-cutting; a college president saying the development fund is lagging; a dry cleaner who is aware that some materials suffer from cleaning. We could list situations by the hundreds—every business or industry has facets where its customers are never quite satisfied. A letter, personal or personalized, is the very best way, next to calls in person, to submit a proposition that will remove that irritation.

PROVE YOUR CLAIM

Many letters do just that. Many advertisements in all media (including TV) do that. But the majority fall down on the "proof." As soon as you have stated your proposition you must justify action. ". . . thus we can assure you that your profits will increase not less than 10 percent with this new line. . . ." Or a power mower dealer might write ". . . due to this new engineering principle that permits cutting almost flush against trees, fences, drives without interrupting cutting . . . we are able to cut the most difficult lawns in at least 20 percent less time than the old-design mowers."

The letter from the manufacturer who will protect profits says:

> You are one of several key dealers in the metropolitan area whose purchases qualify him to represent our Star-Super line, which is being placed on a consignment basis to sell at prices we set as the seller. You act as our agent. . . .

When the consignment-agent relationship is explained, that justifies the claim. Or the design of the lawn-mowers:

> . . . place the wheels fore and aft the cutting blades so that the cutting arc can work within an inch of any solid object . . . .

In a way, the reader who hears or sees something that seems too good to be true—as many letter propositions should be—is looking for the catch. In all business letters to sell, there should be a catch. The proposition would be so attractive, so unusual or so unexpected, that the reader looks for or expects a catch. Technically, we speak of the proposition as the letter's burden. We might add that the proposition and justification are its burden.

LETTER ACCEPTANCE PROBLEMS

Our discussions of burdens have been aimed mostly at reaching heads of companies in industries not familiar with what we stand for, nor with our products. Many larger companies are familiar to thousands of companies with whom they have never had business dealings. Regarding letter acceptance, the well-known company, especially one with a quality reputation (which seems to be a component of longevity) has an entirely different row to hoe. Letters from officers of known companies to counterparts invariably reach their destination. But they die there at rates equal to the unknowns. The advantages enjoyed in getting in can be quickly dissipated by pompous listing of the important companies and other non-essential information—predictions on the rapid rise of the market, etc.

TECHNIQUES FOR KNOWN AND UNKNOWN MAILERS

Even though the letter from a well-known company is assured of a reading, its need for offering to improve a profit situation is as essential as the letter from an unknown. Its greatest advantage, as it is being read, is that it requires less explanation. The unknown makes a statement and then devotes the rest of his time to showing how he can do it. The known company makes a statement and then tells how and why it can be done. The known company writer should inferentially be saying, "as you know." The difference is suggested because it is not flattering to a corporate officer to say, "Coca-Cola is the drink that refreshes. . . ." At the risk of advocating longer sentences, it should read, "As you know, with Coca-Cola's wide reputation as the beverage for the pause that refreshes. . . ." One of the luxuries of a quality reputation is that even industrial buyers may superimpose a high price image on top of your image. Cadillac astutely advertises "costs no more than 15 models of other makes." Quality reputations are buried with many products, but almost all of the older companies in every community are known for quality.

The unfamiliar company should invariably mention users in every commercial letter. Generally the reverse is true for well-known companies. User name listings should be in context at the end of the letter body, directly ahead of the close. In listing users of a product or service in a general mailing to all sizes of companies, care should be observed that more than one half of those listed are as unknown as you are. Most medium and smaller companies are not greatly interested in what the big boys are doing. They often feel that big companies waste money. But do not think you can edify a smaller company by proving that all your clients are unknown. If your user list permits, name one large company for each two smaller unknown companies.

The description of benefits and reasons for the offer will take up most of your letter space. You must have a close to describe how he should get to your cash register. We shall treat that separately in the following brief chapter.

CHAPTER VII

THE LETTER'S CLOSE

Business letters aimed at selling something—a product, service, idea or ideal or the writer himself—cannot leave the results to chance. They must lead the reader to his own payout department. They tell him what to do. That's the close.

We may be breaking a major rule of the letter-writer's union, but we shall start by saying that of the three parts in a business letter, the close is number three in importance. Largely that is because the majority of letters to sell die before they get to the close. As the baseball philosopher is quoted, "There are 85 ways of scoring a run; 10,000 ways of not scoring." All writers recount their winning letters but few really know why they succeeded in a world where losers are the rule.

In essence, the letter's close is almost entirely a technique, as distinguished from the proposition's essence and the justification's factual elements. If a letter were dramatized "live" its close would show it taking the consumer's arm and leading her to the "special offer" or show the busy executive shouting, "Shut off the phones! Stop everything! Get out the red carpet! Get the man who wrote this letter in here!"

THE CLOSE IS THE BECKONING ARM

The letter's close must be entirely the beckoning arm, the road or street map to the bargain counter, or the warm smile of welcome.

Many letters bring good propositions, completely justify action, then blow everything in the final paragraph. The most common way of losing is anxiety. Terms such as "Act now" or "This offer will not be repeated" are examples of anxieties.

Our use of the term "close" in business letters refers to our telling the reader what he does now. It points to his cash register while it says with a smile, "First you pay out, then you put back twice as much." It must give the directions, and it seldom can do much more.

THE CLOSE TELLS READER HOW TO HANDLE YOUR JOB-SEEKING PROPOSITION

The close is not the star of a letter. If kept to its true function it has little part in getting the sale. When the proposition itself and the justification have done their jobs, the close only tells how. In our first selling-yourself letter we said, "If you cannot spare time, I would like to see an associate. . . ." The hidden strength there is that many a favorably received proposition, laid aside until time permits, is easily forgotten or lost. You gave him a way to handle it now. Some writers are offended when shunted to a subordinate. You ask for that.

TECHNIQUES IN CLOSING PERSONAL BUSINESS LETTERS: ASK FOR THE ORDER

As in personal selling, business letters must keep the proposition confined to one way to go, or to a choice between two. This last segment points the way to action. For most letters it is better not to get the sale than to irritate or offend. If a reader is pressured, you not only lose your results, she will avoid visiting your business place.

Always ask for the order. Whoever invented that phrase said it all. The key word is "ask." The technique most effective in closing business letters hinges on helpfulness. There are two simple technique provers for letter closes involving multi-letters:

1. Write your first part and letter body. Then assume the reader immediately has said yes. Now, briefly tell him how to go about buying.

2. Write the close. Omit any substantiation. Just write the close as if he's said "I'll take it."

ONE-SHOT LETTERS TO CONSUMERS AND COMPANIES

Applying these tests to one-shot letters mailed to lists of consumers or companies, the complete and graceful close is, "Just drop the return card in the mail," or whatever natural, easy-to-follow directions are indicated. If you avoid repetition of justification, the close is very brief when one action is selected. Two of the nation's largest mail users recently sent mailings. One went to consumers, the other to retailers. The consumer letter—four pages—from one of the largest publishers closed with, "We'll be looking for your reservation card in the mail. Please send it off today. Thank you. . . ." The letter body closed with ". . . you are never under obligation . . . to purchase books—you may cancel this advance-preview privilege at any time." The other letter, from a large travel-ticket company, closed with, "Take advantage of this offer today . . . the enclosed order form . . . complete and mail today." Both diverted to the card, or form.

Where the letter is not absolutely sure the executive addressed is the proper man, or if your president wants to go through the president to reach a department or staff head, the close might be: 1) pass along to your man who handles; 2) supply me with the name of your executive who handles . . . 3) . . . our representative (or distributor) will be in touch. . . .

CLOSING LETTERS TO TOP EXECUTIVES

When the letter is addressed to the top executive, we have suggested that no enclosures be included. However, very often the purpose of a letter is to transmit a brochure or other printed sales information. In almost every type situation, the letter should be sent separately with the close devoted entirely to the information that the brochure will be along, separately mailed.

The reason for that double-mailing is that a majority of letters that do not reach highly-placed executives are detoured to a department head because an enclosure so indicates. The decision to "route" is based on the secretary's formula of reducing top office mail when it is observed that the material normally goes to purchasing, product planning, financial or another department. Few secretaries read or examine incoming mail beyond the degree necessary to determine proper destination. Despite the difficulty unwanted mail encounters reaching top executives, in larger companies it all gets to some department if it is properly addressed. Usually only the president is hard to reach.

YOUR CLOSE CLASSIFIES YOUR READER

By the time your reader has reached the close of your letter he will have fallen into one of these four classifications: 1) he will act favorably because of a recognized need; 2) he is impressed but far from ready to consider a course of action; 3) he will be disqualified because of a recent purchase, full inventory, availability from regular supplier or any reason not related to the merit of your proposal; 4) he immediately tosses out your letter—no interest. If your letter has been constructed along the lines suggested, those having no interest will be lost at the outset or as they read your justification. The ultimate effectiveness of your letter hinges on its proposition and justification. Your close should make it easy to buy.

TARGETS OF DOOR-OPENING LETTERS

A high percentage of all commercial buying transactions are conducted by professionals in purchasing. Included among those are store owners and general managers in smaller stores and industrial companies. In proposing the letter to a company president from your president as the most desirable level to open doors where you are not now selling, our target is the president of medium and larger companies who normally does not engage in purchasing decisions. In instances where top management is engaged in purchasing, commercial letters will reach them easier. But the degree of burden on the close will be greater. The top officer who hears all supplier offerings takes them in stride. He may have staff people who examine proposals such as yours, with a result that he remains unaware. On balance, the effectiveness of a commercial letter as it relates to the size of organization cannot be estimated.

CLOSING COMMERCIAL LETTERS TO RETAILERS

The rule of thumb for business letters to retailers is that in smaller companies the president and other top echelons are interested in every aspect of the business on a day-to-day basis. In the larger companies we assume that the president and some top specialists devote their time to policy or events in their specialized fields. If a manufacturer issues a "line closeout" bulletin it would not normally go to these. Those executives directly concerned with buying and selling are on the lookout for all dollars and cents announcements. Their mail is loaded with "profit opportunities."

AVOID JUSTIFYING IN YOUR CLOSE

Keep in mind that all business letters normally go between counterparts. Letters from factory marketing vice presidents on a new line or new models may be larded with product and price philosophy, but they also must tell which present models are superseded and how much the prices are changed. In all types of business—large or small—owners, managers and presidents are concerned with building the business when things are on the upbeat; when things slow down their interest is in inventory and turnover. Always profits. Profit is the key word to all customers. With consumers the key word is savings. Letter writers are usually fully aware of those keys, but they tend to include elements of their justification in the close of their letters.

CLOSING COMPANY-TO-COMPANY LETTERS

There is no rule that says "proof" (justification) must be confined to one paragraph. The two- three- and four-page letters (very common for selling items to "verbal" markets) usually put their proposition in one sentence, then three-plus pages of description or verbal embellishment. The close is, "For your convenience . . . reservation card. . . ." A management company-to-company letter's close hinges upon two broad conditions: 1) policy level letters must work, they must ask the reader to do something, delegate something to a department head, supply us with name of man to see, permit us to visit his office, etc.; 2) letters to department heads (merchandisers, engineers, purchasing, financial) ask for an interview when "in the neighborhood with our distributor," enclose return card to get brochure, ask for OK to "drop into the office when nearby."

WHEN TO ENCLOSE PRINTED LITERATURE

Letters in the second category probably should have enclosed a selected piece of literature that fits into a standard size envelope. The letters themselves are 90 percent public relations. The PR reason for such letters is that all retail department heads like advance word on big moves of their supplier factories. To some extent recipients of letters in the first category are pleased at personal word from the head of a national company. The close is how they do what you are writing about. It is often good strategy to start commercial letters ". . . before we release it to the press. . . ." But after you have told him the new models are coming and explained where they fit into the dealer's inventory and profit pattern, you ask (in your close) that he do something, as in the examples.

THE CLOSE IS THE WORK ASSIGNMENT

In the foregoing examples of the close of commercial letters between factories and stores, our aim is to illustrate and emphasize that every letter must work, that the close is the work assignment. That is true of all business letters. The return card and the redemption coupon are the common denominators of most business letters today. For letters from top executives on the president's letterhead the return card often is engraved on white stock, if there is an invitation involved.

Staff writers in large companies or agencies may compose letters for four or five levels of signatures for a single new model program. These would range from such bread and butter items as the bulletins outlining "stock orders" to the sales manager's letter suggesting selling devices and tricks. In larger companies the president's office usually confines its letter ghosting to his secretary or staff assistants. When the marketing department has a capable writer his help may be welcome.

FUND RAISING LETTERS

Switching to a letter situation where the writer is an alumni committee member seeking funds, the close is slightly different. Generally the original announcements of the "drive" involve meetings. When letters are used at that time, it is suggested that they state the proposition, justify it, then say ". . . in the next few days I shall call your office to verify your luncheon meeting reservation. I am confining this group to some whose presence will be effective—there will be no fund solicitation at the meeting." Here we believe a return card makes it too easy to duck the meeting. As the drive progresses most development funds employ publicity and a series of letters to keep the members informed. When writers have reports of progress to tell, the letters can be meaty, and they might attach coupons to return indicating pledges.

In using a ". . . for your convenience . . ." type close, you must be extremely careful that it does not boomerang to become an easy out. An example might be a letter asking for funds (alumni) with a pledge card. If a liberal giver is permitted to fill out his own card alone, you may lose money.

ANOTHER LOOK AT EXECUTIVE EMPLOYMENT LETTERS

For a final note on this third element in letters, we might take another look at your close on a letter seeking executive employment. You have written your proposition, explained your basic qualifications for an appointment and now you want to close the letter to bring an invitation to come in. ". . . I would appreciate a personal interview with you. In the event that it could not fit into your busy schedule, it might be possible for me to see an associate. In either case, I shall be available at whatever time meets your convenience. Sincerely yours."

When an employed executive writes on his own stationery asking an employment interview, he should not give his company telephone number. His home address, but not his phone number, appears at the letter's head. He should not mention that "this is in confidence." Even if he might expect his recipient to call him, he should not suggest it. His name should be in the directory. The insertion of the word "personal" might be negative, but it is recommended for two reasons: 1) you don't want the letter going to the personnel department and 2) you immediately say "or an associate."

SUMMARIZING THE LETTER'S CLOSE

The close should not be a slight progression from the basic reasons you qualify. End the justification before you start to tell how to proceed. If you fail to clearly separate these, the reader is not conscious of making a decision on a second step—how he does something. The perfect close is the one that merely implies, "Now you know what you are offered. Now you must decide if you want to hear more."

CHAPTER VIII

LETTERS TO GET BUSINESS FOR SMALLER RETAILERS AND SERVICE STORES

Generally speaking, few smaller retailers advertise much outside their stores. Service dealers, often seeking business passed up by chains and bigger stores, are well-suited to directories—telephone and newspaper. In fields inhabited by national brands, notably such home items as electric appliances and housewares, TV-radio, garden and lawn power equipment, the factories usually prepare mailing materials on a shared cost basis. Sometimes they even handle the mailing. In various patterns some form of the above applies to men's wear, soft and chaise-type furniture and almost everything where the price is $25 or more. But only a genius could write personalized letters to fit conditions in several thousand stores.

CAPITALIZING ON PERSONAL RELATIONS OPPORTUNITIES

The dealer whose type of business involves purchases of more than $25, or whose sales are put on travel-credit or factory credit cards should write a letter to his customers and others at least four times annually, sticky though the task may be. Often he is in direct competition with large stores carrying the same lines. Their advertising can blanket the community, but he can reach his projected market by limited mailings to familiar and nearby prospects and customers. The larger store lacks his personal opportunities. In calls upon 110 smaller to medium size sales and service stores with the question, "Do you ever send letters or mailings to your customers?" the majority said "yes." "Do you ever write them personal business letters, self-composed?" Only two said they used any planned, self-written letters. Fourteen others said they had tried, "but it didn't work for me."

Department and furniture stores often have public relations letters aimed at personalizing the store. What works for them often works even better where the personal touch is not synthetic. The big local image stores are capitalizing on a relationship not available to chains and discounters. However, even with its second and third generation charge accounts and its customer saturation in a fifty-mile radius, the big store's major promotion is through daily papers; and their best buy is the maximum use of enclosed folders with monthly statements.

Smaller stores with the personal relationships of the owners in the community can make planned personal business letters their major trade stimulator. The fact that you can send a single letter, or 10 or more daily, makes it ideal for thanking new customers or keeping in touch with lesser-seen older ones. For major purchases such as TV, stereo, furniture, carpeting and appliances, department stores have a "president's letter" that re-assures the householder who recently signed a payment contract. But the vast majority of smaller dealers depend upon in-person relationships even though most agree that they see most customers only occasionally.

LETTERS TO RE-ESTABLISH OVER-DUE ACCOUNT CUSTOMERS

Considering each dealer's own list as his best, we shall discuss three types of letters that should pay their way if used in the proposed highly personal manner. These are: 1) to recapture old customers seldom seen recently, 2) to sell a specific service or product with special offer, 3) to resurrect former customers who have past due bills and now buy less often.

Large companies with professional credit departments have made a fine art of chasing over-due bills by mail. Only a handful of smaller stores and professional men are even acquainted with the art. Their theory appears to be that if the delinquent will not pay when he passes the store daily, a letter will not jog loose the money. Without arguing that subject, we shall suggest such a letter.

Dear Mr. Brown:

Because I haven't seen you lately I am writing to ask if our service has been careless or otherwise below expectations. I noticed on our books that we have not received your remittances lately, not a serious oversight but perhaps a sign of a service lapse on our part.

As you know, we value your business very highly. If we have missed the mark in performance, I'd like to know because it may be taking your business elsewhere. With regard to your unpaid balance here, please be assured that you are entitled to whatever leeway is your pleasure. Frankly, we have some months when we get a little extra time from our suppliers.

Meanwhile, as a personal matter I would like to know if we have fallen down. When we do not have visits from a valued customer, that is a matter I want to straighten out. Won't you give me a call, or drop in?

Best personal regards,

Sincerely yours,
John Smith, Manager

Some may say that we are "turning the other cheek." We will say only this: never write a letter that does not aim to improve a relationship. You can make enemies and estrangements in easier ways. Slow pays are a part of doing business on credit. Yet, unless the customer is alienated, more than 95 percent of these finally pay. Even though an all-is-forgiven letter loses the unpaid bill, you stand to re-establish the customer on a cash basis. You will observe that the above opening statement gets directly to our proposition. You want him to come back. The trite ". . . you have overlooked . . ." is omitted. Almost all delinquent bills in neighborhoods are due to money shortages. Families with over-burdening bills will pay some, skip others. Some learn to live that way and it includes avoiding creditors. You have a better chance for payment if they return, than if they stay away.

In our second paragraph (justification) you bluntly say that you want his present business ". . . you are entitled to . . . leeway . . . we get a little extra time from our suppliers." That is strong justification for the customer.

Your present request for a call or "... drop in ..." should erase any guilt feeling.

HOW TO ATTRACT INFREQUENT CUSTOMERS

Another source of potential sales from letters is the type aimed at increasing the frequency of visits from seldom seen customers. We should start by carefully examining our supply of product literature from several manufacturers, or from the supply source of our main commodities: travel folders, carpeting brochures, power outdoor equipment, electronic home-goods or soft goods such as draperies, outerwear, etc. We are going to recommend enclosing one folder instead of two or more. We want our letter to be the star of this project. And we want it oriented to both our service and sales. We will first analyze our strongest competitive potential. Let us start with this. Retailers need not be cautioned to adhere closely to seasonal patterns. Holiday gifts and customs are dominant factors in selling items used by the family or in the home. Every product that can be fitted into a box or other package encloses a warranty of some kind. Most good salesmen use its provisions to help close the sale. How many dealers ever mention it to the buyer? That question was asked of most of the 110 appliance dealers recently surveyed. Most of them just smiled. A few said, "we fix any complaint." Of those asked more than half said, "we send them back to the factory." Eighteen provided some service, mostly for TV or radio. But not one recalls ever writing a letter "asking for trouble." Almost to a store they criticized and disliked a big chain store that "just knocks the market to pieces," as one dealer said. Most dealers are familiar with the money back practices of national chains. We will try both sales and service appeals. Here is an example:

Dear Mrs. Jones:

Several of your electric appliances have been in service for two to ten years according to our records. The data here shows that they are quality purchases, so you perhaps have not needed repairs or adjustments. To become re-acquainted, we are offering a special conditioning and cleaning bargain. We will supply the labor to recondition any three portable appliances for $9.50, plus the cost of whatever parts need replacement. Or, if you want this treatment for one appliance, it will cost $5.00. Normally the reconditioning cost per appliance is $7.50.

The only limitation on our offer is: you must notify us within 10 days of the date of this letter. We will tell you when and how long your item will be away. We are doing this now because our shop can devote the time, and we believe it is good business for us to assure further long service to your appliances. I am enclosing a folder showing our new DeLuxe power mowers that we now have at a special price.

If we can recondition one, three or any number of your appliances, please call Miss Smith at MA 7-9432. She will make arrangements for the pickup and return.

Yours very truly,

Two immediate comments on this letter are: families that own long-lasting appliances never forget where they bought them. Dealers do forget. They even exhibit suspicion that the appliance is a ringer when it comes in for repairs. Second, if your letterhead is moderately attractive, most women will read it, primarily because they know you.

POTENTIAL OF LETTERS TO BUILD BUSINESS: THE TRAVEL AGENCY

Suppose you have a travel agency:

Dear Mr. Smith:

Proposition:

While it is still several months before you will be aboard a super-jet winging South for the winter vacation, I am concerned whether we can get your accommodations when it's time. To meet this situation, I am now placing some tentatitve stops on some facilities that would include providing yours. Without suggesting that you make definite reservations now, it might be mutually helpful if you could tell us if you plan something different the coming season. If I recall rightly, you were pleased with our former arrangements.

Justification:

According to the trade press, projections are that this season's Southern business will represent continuation of the uptrend. That reflects a customer benefit because costs in vacation facilities tend to level where volume increases. Meanwhile, even more than in some years, a considerable number of new facilities are available. Far from wishing to hurry you, it would be helpful if we had a word on your present inclination or of your specific plans, including place and time.

Close:

For your convenience I am enclosing a "tentative blocking" reservation card. Of course, no obligation is involved. Just check your intention and drop the card in the mail.

This sample letter is presented complete because of a unique marketing situation. The Travel Agency is a new industry with deep personal ties with its customers. Built on the "back to the old country" and the "around the world" luxury, the modern travel office offers one highly personal and friendly link in a world where strangers dominate.

Very few of these new "friendly ports" are aggressive in going after business. Yet even as they are increasingly noticing the overcrowding of travel offices in some neighborhoods and the entry of big stores to the field, they contentedly say that office location is 90 percent of a successful start. As smaller service retailers, they represent prime examples of wasting a heritage. Travel arranging is a highly personal business. The agent's personality is the number one reason for dealing with one instead of another. But most of them risk their futures upon literature—brochures, folders and maps—supplied by airlines and resorts to all agents. It is not suggested that the agencies seek "private label" facilities, but they are heading for the time when travel facilities and arrangement services will be in oversupply. There is no better example of the potential of letters than in this new service business. Almost every type of smaller retailer of commodities and services for the home and family found a crowded field when he entered the business. Automotive service facilities might rank highest in over-availability looked at socially in a specific neighborhood. But complete data shows that as the nation's biggest—in dollars available for purchasing—automotive related businesses are among the most indestructible. That indicates they are not generally in over-supply.

MOTIVATING NEW MARKETS BY PERSONAL SERVICE AND LETTERS

In rating aviation-related services to automotive, we have the extremes—polar extremities—of acceptance. In use-acceptance, autos have 100 percent. In that same vein, aviation facilities are used by less than 20 percent. The business-building opportunity of travel agencies through personal media—letters, personal calls and the telephone—is partially due to the carrier's almost universal affliction of public utility promotion-blindness. The travel agent must motivate new markets (other than business travel and some bland resort tie-ins) if his business is to remain solvent in the face of an increase of 50 percent to 150 percent in his neighborhood. He is the only friendly face vacationists ever see in the market place. The cause of his need for highly personalized marketing is that the carriers have abandoned planned passenger acceptance. Their best efforts are 90 percent inbred. They are aware that under Governmental regulations they can thrive without risk of newcomers to the industry by getting their share of existing business between almost any combination of key cities. This is reflected in advertising aimed at attractive planes and hostesses and other embellishments appealing to existing markets but lost on non-users.

The summary of the weak role of air carriers in developing new business may be over-simplified, but it is accurate in its reflection upon the position of the travel agencies. Almost without exception, astute agency operators are neglecting their own futures if they pass a single day without reaching out the personal hand of service and friendship. As smaller retailers, letters are by far their best communications method because only one out of five wants their product.

PERSONALIZED PROCESS LETTERS

Retailers often tell of mailings that cost them too much and got them nothing. In our recent (110 dealers) survey, one dealer outlined a 10 month co-op activity conducted with a TV distributor. He imprinted a message in simulated longhand on the face of an attractive letter size product folder. Three hundred of these were mailed monthly to the best homes in his 65,000 suburban Eastern city. His cost was $65 monthly, mostly to pay for his imprinted message. An example of one well-reproduced message is:

> Everyone knows where Jay's TV Sales and Service is located: right opposite St. Luke's church on Ogden Avenue. I've arranged with the world's best electronics manufacturer, Superba Products, to send

you monthly reminders that we value your patronage. We consider ourselves your neighbor. Friendly integrity is our business. Whether for repairs, or for that new DeLuxe color set, we would welcome a call or a visit. . . .

                        (signed)
                             Jay

Perhaps that is too lame for comment. We are not sure that he had a genuine objective that would motivate his customers. As a practical matter, never assume, in writing or speech, that anyone knows where your store is located. If you want to experiment, stand on a corner near your store and ask passers-by where your store location is.

In looking at several of the product folders that Jay used they were seen to be attractive and appeared well-conceived. The cost of the mailings would have been approximately the same if Jay had used personalized processed letters. An advantage would have been that Jay would have established an objective for each mailing. That appears to be the missing link.

Dear Mrs. Jackson:

Proposition:

Now that color TV sets have come into free supply, we are planning to continue the home-engineering installations we originated two years ago when there was a color set shortage. This service provides for an unqualified home free trial, regardless of whether you choose our Superba Compact Tru-Color set at $349 or one of Superba's deluxe units. Our TV engineer prescribes room location, antenna modification and other facets to assure fine performance.

Justification:

During the two years when high quality electronics manufacturers such as Superba were installing limited numbers of sets in homes across the nation, the final touches to bring their exclusive Tru-Color were tested in homes. Now that all materials, both imported and domestic, are in free supply for color manufacture, our customers will find available models with months of home performance tests behind them, including those selling in a price range similar to black and white sets.

Close:

Enclosed is the brochure on the Model XX Compact. It is one of 18 models comprising the line Superba is producing. Also your free home trial reservation card is enclosed. Please mark it and drop it in the mail now. It involves no purchase obligation, but it assures you immediate home-trial installation whenever you call or visit the store.

DEALING WITH MERCHANDISING SHORTAGES

One of the most perplexing characteristics of all types of retail business is how to deal with merchandise shortages in specific lines. Large dealers and small alike may be out of the item, or, on items where sales run ahead of production, "We couldn't be able to make delivery until after Christmas." When a product goes through a long term shortage period, such as happened with color TV in the mid-1960's, or as happens repeatedly with some automobile models, we should consider applying our technique to mollify disappointed shoppers.

> Dear Mrs. Johnson:
>
> It has come to my attention that your recent inquiry for an item in our home furnishings department found us unable to show what you were looking for. When a customer of our store does not find what she came in for, we regret it very much, and I think we owe you an explanation.
>
> As you know, the product you sought is imported. A year ago when we made our commitment for this year's supply from the factory we anticipated a strong demand because of that line's unusual appeal. Our shipments arrived on time and in the quantities we ordered. Someplace we underestimated the demand. With much of the season well ahead, our supply is depleted. We have been offered substitutes, but we prefer to wait a few weeks until we can replenish this line.
>
> As soon as our receiving dates for these items are confirmed, we will notify you immediately. I hope that this will not inconvenience you too greatly.
>
> Sincerely yours,
>
> _____
> President

The letter from the head of the business telling a disappointed shopper that we regret not having an item she asked for can delay her shopping elsewhere and it can make a lasting friend. She will show the letter around. Families that buy imports in design equipment make buying decisions on a longer basis than average bargain seekers.

LETTERS TO HANDLE CUSTOM MODEL SHORTAGES

High class stores selling television and phonograph quality lines draw a higher percentage of home furnishings seekers than average dealers. Partially as a result of its long shortage period when it was new, color TV dealers tend to emphasize low-end models of standard lines and limited displays of custom (luxury) models of lines supporting these high-end models with national advertising. When a shopper shows interest in custom models, he is shown the model in the line brochure. We do not urge dealers to be adamant about ". . . our next shipment . . ." and taking the name and phone number. But quality high-end sales beget high-end sales, so we suggest that this situation be met aggressively.

> Dear Mrs. Jackson:
>
> It came to my attention that when you recently visited our store we were unable to show you a Caxton Cabinet Superba color TV set. I wish to apologize for that situation. We have no excuse in that we knew our customers would choose that model because it is outstanding. I have just been in touch with the factory and am informed that every effort is being made to have these models in our store within a very short time.
>
> As you will recall, there was a time when shoppers waited for whatever model color TV set became available. With the demand for utilitarian units, Superba's facilities for producing its famous custom models were not expanded in keeping with the market increase. Their schedules for these hand-finished, fine furniture models are now increased, but it seems that they have not yet caught up with orders.
>
> As soon as we have shipping notice on this unit you will be notified. I sincerely hope that it does not inconvenience you too much.
>
> Sincerely yours,

――――――――――
President

When a customer is disappointed the value of a letter of apology from the head of the company increases by multiples where other lines are also merchandised. The personal letter will do its job even if the customer has bought elsewhere.

CHAPTER IX

THE SHORT LETTER WITH THE STRONG PROPOSITION

The Inter-Office Memo

It may not be a peculiarly American institution, but the inter-office memo is by all odds the most powerful and widely-used person to person message form in the history of business. Once its function was served largely by answers scribbled across letter-bottoms or on note paper, fragments clipped to subject letters, meetings and even by trips. Now the office memo has a life of its own, and often absolute acceptance as the company record. Its usages change from company to company, but its patterns are formal within each. Where it is widely encouraged as the substitute for meetings, and even long-winded phone calls, it may be taken for granted, but it never goes unread. Perhaps its greatest recent gain is its current acceptance for inter-company communications simulated as commercial letters.

HISTORY OF THE OFFICE MEMO

The history of the office memo is vague. Its use as a file reference record may have ascended as many organizations used it as a committee post-meeting summary. From there it was just a step to "interim reports" and to the variety of updating common in organizations with such multiple activities as advance planning and other committee projects. Strategically it is a powerful tool. No one leaves his office for the day leaving behind an unread memo in his mail basket. Especially if it is green—or whatever color the big boss uses. Larger company executives are familiar with and respectful of the often garish, usually square—pink, yellow, brown—with names, departments, subjects and functions neatly outlined at the top of memos that must be read. From trainees to top officer's corner suite, executives have come to judge each other on their memo proficiency. In a given company there often is a striking similarity of technique. Above all, at almost every level, the memo is a recurring opportunity to exhibit one's communications skills. This is especially true for the younger men.

ADVANTAGES OF THE MEMO FOR EFFECTIVE COMMUNICATIONS

The memo had an original advantage that it has improved upon. It required setting apart at its top such data as subject, time, place and numerous fringe facts. That left the writer face to face with his bare proposition as his starting point. The memo's immense present place in corporations and departmental communications blossomed when corporate diversifications, new product planning and other organizational innovations multiplied the need for meetings and travel. A memo is quicker than a meeting or a trip.

With few temptations to startle or arouse the reader, the office memo is recognized by many as the most effective communications technique business has evolved. The fact that it plays only to captive audiences is a point in its favor as a technique available for commercial and consumer letters. Quite apart from internal company letters, the short letter has always been the prevailing technique in the competitive business world. Only the more sophisticated letter writers often use two, three or four pages. All letters are applications of techniques varying to suit the subject and the reader. So it was inevitable that memos, almost unfailingly effective, would become patterns. Indirectly, their ownership of a captive reader points up the necessity of leverage and their position in context of continuing in-company projects where existing pre-knowledge is a part of the situation points up the need for close study of the reader's pre-knowledge of product, service or writer's company for business letters.

SHORT CONSUMER LETTERS CARRY A SPECIFIC OFFER

In this discussion of shorter (page or less) letters, we shall not overlook that their length hinges upon the proposition (or product) and the reader (his relationship to proposition). Omitting transmittal and other non-letter letters, we must consider the letter itself as the burden-carrier, although in personal business and consumer letters, retailers will usually enclose a product-folder. The short consumer letter should bring a definite offering—preferably one that saves money for the family. One way of wasting money is to generalize about plenty of parking, the friendly welcome, etc. It has been said that short letters are easy to write if you have the time. We shall paraphrase that. Short letters are easy to write if you keep several typical interoffice memos in front of you. None of these dare come up empty.

VALUE YOUR RESPECTED NAME

While our prototype, the office memo, is skin-tight, it is the ultimate example of the importance of an influential name, and it refutes for all time the delicate notion that writers should talk about "you" instead of "I". The big boss starts his memos "I would like to see . . ." and it always happens that way. A good dealer offering a bargain in a letter to neighbors starts, "I am offering a money saving . . ." or "I have made a fortunate purchase that I would like to pass on. . . ." That dealer has his personality, his civic position, and his integrity—all elements that the chain or discount store can seldom produce "in person."

TECHNIQUES AND TABOOS IN EFFECTIVE SHORT LETTER WRITING

Our aim is far from attempting to sell short letters as preferable to long ones. Using the office memo as our stereotype, we will discuss short letters involving techniques; forms and contents that give them power. Short letters trying to communicate complex or involved propositions can put you out of the letter-writing business. The short letter has lots in common with those requiring several pages, but violations of taboos in short letters will nullify your efforts faster. Here are five taboos.

Don't 1) repeat statements from earlier correspondence; 2) write statements of fact that have appeared in the newspapers or trade press; 3) start your letter with an attention-getter (the proposition comes first); 4) withdraw or qualify your proposition by any disclaimer after it has been stated; 5) restate your proposition at the close. Just refer back for reference. In speeches, instructional media and other forms a favorite closing gambit is to "tell them what you told them." In letters you tell them where and how to get it.

In restricting this discussion to shorter letters—single paragraph or two paragraph letters—we obviate some recommended practices for letters requiring longer treatments. Because the reader can see the entire proposition, justification and close at one time, these need not be set down one, two, three, as where the reader makes judgments as he reads. That does not mean that a majority of the formula restraints applying to business letters can be abandoned by any given type of letter. As mentioned earlier, when using inter-office memos as our prototype we must be highly aware of the power of leverage in our proposition. In inter-office communications the leverage is the memo's potential for updating the reader on essential information. Likewise, the essential degree of pre-knowledge in short letters is invariably greater than in complex letters. If you write ". . . now we have on our floor full displays of color TV . . ." the reader shrugs and opens the next letter.

THE POWER OF LEVERAGE IN COMMERCIAL LETTERS

Commercial letters fail more often due to lack of leverage in the proposition, regardless of the ultimate length of the letter, than for lack of brevity or conviction. When a busy executive receives a personal business letter (written by a contemporary) he either reads it until he loses interest, or he has someone he pays to do that. That is the basic cause for the longer letter for communicating between companies with selling propositions. Once that is understood, we should evaluate the burden of our commercial letters before we determine their length. If we are writing to a customer, the first question may be: Does this officer know that his company buys supplies from us? Does he know that he (his company) is a member of our organization? Does he know what we do for them? When you can assume "yes" in answer to these questions you can state your proposition without reference to existing relationships. In a commercial letter to a buyer, or to a smaller company official of a present customer, you always avoid such references as ". . . being a long-time customer of. . . ."

SPECIALIZED BUSINESS LETTERS

We shall discuss some types of specialized business letters separately because all of these do not follow blanket rules. For example, stockholders and employees have their own language in relationship to the company. To stockholders we may be ". . . your company"; to employees we are ". . . the company." That rather thin slicing of audience differences is highly familiar to executives for internal writing. When their letters go outside the company, even among old customers or association members, they lose that fine sense of the reader's preknowledge. And that loss takes away their sound of sincerity and good taste. Often they mistakenly forego saying something impressive or cute—and when the letter reaches the reader, it sounds stupid.

HANDLING CUSTOMER INQUIRIES

When a customer writes in for information, regardless of type of company, your answer almost never should be more than one hundred words. If it takes more than that it should be on a piece of printed literature, or a representative should go see him or phone him. If he asks a single question, your answer is a memo-type letter.

KEEP UP-TO-DATE ON COMPANY AND COMPETITIVE ACTIVITIES

As we proceed with these discussions of writing techniques suited to specific business situations you will observe that only rarely do we discuss two-way, or answer letters. This discussion of short letters represents most of our experience and research on that subject. In placing our memo writer in a big business context, we are aiming at showing how he learned to write memos. Once any writer understands that viewpoint he knows what he should for back and forth letters. If a staff member in a large organization misses several meetings of a committee, the theory is that he gets up to date by reviewing the resulting memos. Should he omit this homework and dictate a long memo to those who had attended, he could be in trouble. That situation, in the larger field of inter-company or consumer communications, very often exists without the letter writer being aware. He has a new model or a new product in his line, and he writes to his best customers listing advantages that the competition has had for months or years.

GETTING INTERVIEWS WITH ONE PARAGRAPH LETTERS

As the classic form of short letters in business, the inter-office memo can well be the prototype for all short letters, but the situation must be a single category, or very limited subject letter. Assuming that all products are equipped with brochures or product advance information folders aimed at your prime customer, salesmen sending such information to the executives they would call on should use a memo, or brief letter, to convoy that literature. However, if he is aware that the product description sounds like any model in the industry, he should avoid sending the "me too" folders. In keeping with his personal standing, he preferably would simply ask for appointments in one paragraph letters.

SEPARATE PRODUCT AND SERVICE IN SELLING LETTERS

When stores with service departments write selling letters it is well to separate product and service. Most retailers have service in some form, but they have little beyond their willingness and personal service attitude to distinguish them from a competitor. When a customer in a TV-radio store looks at one model, she has no overwhelming sense of wanting it unless she knows it is being offered at 25 percent off. The dealer cannot do anything to enhance the appeal of that one model. But he can talk about "in-home performance our engineers bring by proper installations." Also, he can show a hundred sets stacked to the ceiling, several brands so she can choose among them with a feeling that she is seeing everything in the market. The dealer should send her a letter as a follow-up, short and easy to read, saying, "come in and see the new arrivals in the full line of new Deluxe Brand TV color sets. . . ." Nothing would happen if she had not already learned of his big stock—that is what brings her back. But if a shopper sees a hundred models and continues to shop elsewhere, the dealer's best saver to rekindle her interest would be a short note emphasizing some reduced prices. That is not the time for a long letter saying she got more for her money when she bought at his store.

We have mentioned two types of situations where short letters work effectively: 1) with single ideas, and answers to written inquiries and 2) where we emphasize a single element (such as price).

EMPHASIZE A SINGLE ELEMENT IN BRIEF LETTERS TO CUSTOMERS

The second type, emphasizing a single element, fits well for any retailer as a personal business letter to shoppers disappointed at not finding a major item of clothing, household goods or construction materials on a store visit.

> Dear Mrs. Jones:
>
> I have heard that you did not find the merchandise you were shopping for recently at our store and I hope you will accept my apology and regrets. It is our pride that we have more than adequate stocks of everything we carry, but sometimes shortages or mis-shipments prevail.
>
> I have asked Miss Frances in our Customers' Relations office to be on the lookout so that it does not happen again. Would you please call her when you are coming in again for a major item? If it is

not in stock in the specific item fitting your need, she will alert you and tell you when it will be here.

Yours truly,

_____
President

This example of a short letter would pre-suppose that sales personnel reported on a form items asked for but not present. It is not strictly a selling letter, nor does it follow the usual form. The use of the first person, and the president's signature, are its strong points for big stores. This is a one-shot situation letter. It is not involved in any way with any series that is underway. One-shots must deal with specifics. Occasional general letters for prestige or other public relations benefits must be scheduled as is the employees publication.

THE BARGAIN LETTER—A ONE-SHOT SITUATION

A special letter may be the consumer letter—personalized or "Dear Neighbor." Or, it may be a personal business letter such as the above. Again using TV sets sales and service as our example (they are prone to service beefs) let us devise a consumer letter offering a bargain. The rule is that series-letters expect no action. One-shot offers such as this are failures if they do not get action. Letters offering bargains should be short. If the reader is not interested, don't hold her. Generally speaking, when you have a bargain in a product, if you made a purchase not duplicated by competition, you should advertise it in your windows and the newspaper. Confine letter bargains to service and other personal aspects of your business. Letters for retailers suffering out of date images, such as "old-line," "solid price" "fair trade," etc. can cut deeply into such price competition as chains and discount stores. The dealer-operated store with its own service should promote it in letters, in keeping with the personal nature of that capability. Short letters offering service bargains are effective for furs and other high price wearables, home equipment including decorator materials, appliances and radio-TV, stereo and dozens of items where making it workable is more important than money back.

Dear Neighbor:

During August, prior to our busy season, I am offering a money-saving television complete overhaul; repair, clean and adjust for the special price of $9.50. At regular rates these overhauls average $16. We would keep your set three days, and return it working as it did when new.

Because our facilities have limits, we shall not advertise this offer. I am writing to a few neighbors whose overhauls will use our slack time in August. Should your set need a new part we would install and adjust it without added labor cost if you gave your approval. When your set is restored, we will deliver it, adjust it to your room, check and adjust your antenna. Your total bill will be $9.50.

If you would like us to pick it up, please call me at 567-0275. My office will tell you when we will come.

Yours truly,

Women have faith in "out of season" buys. Also, they read all money-saving offers. Offers of bargains do not need personalized letters. Letters for public relations, in series, must be personalized. In sending letters that could snow you under it is well to start with limited daily mailings. Increase or cut as returns indicate.

CHAPTER X

YOUR PERSONALITY IN THE BUSINESS LETTER

Our interest in personality is entirely as it reflects in the business letter. That usually is only remotely related to one's in-person charm, friendly smile or winning way. The letter carrying an appeal over the signature of a well-known fund administrator would be based on the validity and urgency of the need. Although irrelevant, before signing off he would mention tax deduction. These factors reflect the established character of the writer. He is known to business men as reliable. "Givers" also know his reputation for responsible fund handling. The letter bearing his signature must hew closely to that character.

We might give further examples, such as the conservative politician who writes to constituents that an opposition project is a raid on the treasury, or a college prexy fronting for the development fund to broaden the scholarship program. All of these are extensions of established personalities. Their letters' propositions are expected— in character—their prose style is unchanging. This strongly implies the personality influence. But most of us are not politicians, leaders nor educators with known programs. We do not have a personality such as might be evoked by the signature "Foxy Grandpa." So, the starting point for the personality we reflect must be related to the stereotype for the ideal already established in the mind of the reader.

FIT YOUR IDEAL PROFESSIONAL IMAGE

Our definition of business letter personality is a letter that fits the ideal image of the office it comes from whether it be a president, financial officer, marketer or engineer. That may sound elemental because it is the aim of most staff writers and many executives. When an executive moves up from v.p. marketing to the presidency his language changes. He wants to become a business statesman. Careerists such as engineers are less prone to make concessions to stereotypes. This may not damage their business letters if it makes them sound more like engineers. To inject personality factors we must emphasize language that strikes a familiar response in our reader. In commercial letters that pass between contemporaries—president to president, engineer to engineer and salesmen to buyers—there is an empathy. Their viewpoints are shaped by the same occupational pressures—such as costs, quality, inventories, one-time deliveries, etc.

PERSONALITY IN CONSUMER LETTERS

Consumer letters (mass mailings) gain personality through just showing the president's signature. But consumers are cagy—they have ideas of how a president sounds. They often sense the spurious. When they see an endorsement by a celebrity in a magazine it had better be compatible: athletes praising outdoor products or handsome actors showing men's clothes. The most striking example of the personality creation is the cartoon or comic strip character. Popeye and spinach; Hoppy and fair play; Peanuts and wisdom.

Most letter writers cannot shift titles and occupations as easily as the radio story teller becomes "Uncle Benny" or the car salesman the "Happy Swede." Fiction writers usually portray the corporate hierarchy as strictly stuffed shirts. That is accomplished by their actions, ideas and language. In letter writing, these higher ups tend to use stilted, overly-formal language unconsciously, and their expressed ideas often are consciously conservative. This applies to many executives in marketing, finance and the other functional departments.

LANGUAGE CREATES READER IMPRESSIONS

For business letter purposes we should envision ourselves as the signers, giving the reader an image of our personalities without resorting to biographical notes. That personality could be for us what the jingle is to the TV commercial or the logotype to a print advertisement. Something in our language or expression that gives the stranger-reader an impression; or when repeated in later letters, identifies you and supplies continuity.

We all agree frequently that the letter is the most personal of all communications used for business. By seeking to inject some personality factors we get the benefits of that intimacy. Politicians, cause-leaders, athlete-businessmen and other public figures are often combinations of what is heard, seen or read. They may speak over the radio or be seen speaking on TV, or their statements may be printed in the newspapers. In the "live" appearance they smile, scowl or posture. These diversions reduce the impact of their ideas. When those ideas are in cold print, they may stamp him as a lightweight, stuffed shirt or a wise man.

DETERMINE A WRITER-READER RELATIONSHIP FOR IMPACT

When we write letters we do not have access to "live" exposure to our readers. We must create, for one individual, an impact resembling to some degree the impingement of other attention-seekers ranging from public figures to in-person salesmen. Our letters to homes, if we are a retail store in the community, must fully utilize the chance of stamping personality to offset concurrent and competing radio, newspaper and TV selling appeals.

Let us put our discussion into the context of a letter to customers that may be handled by the executive, whatever his function, or by a staff writer for the executive signature. The first need is for a point of view. Determine your relationship to the reader. Isolate one reader. If necessary, write a short profile of him. Job? Lives where? Married? Duties at job, etc? Think of him as a man you meet at your club. You should treat him in what you feel to be your most effective manner to get the conversation around to telling him you want to do business with him.

CONSTRUCTING PRESIDENT-STATUS LETTERS

When a sales writer prepares a letter for the president's signature, it is sometimes difficult to phrase it so that it does not sound or read as if the president were also the sales promotion manager. At the risk of dwelling on detail, it is suggested that marketing writers submit the proposition write-up to the president and ask him to dictate his views briefly "to supply something to go on."

ORGANIZE AND RESEARCH "PROPOSITION" MEMOS

The ideal and only sure method of proceeding on such a letter is to first organize a proposition memo. As a practical matter, it would be a lot more to the point if it were circulated for approvals. Then when all were agreed, the writer would get out the letter, injecting the president's personality.

The president-status letter should have a formally researched proposition. The sales head should assign, or himself write the memorandum stating the proposition. For a new product that memo might read:

"To cover all bases, we should get out some letters to 1) field organization, 2) distributors, 3) customers and 4) a trade list, giving them a pre-announcement of our new portable heater before trade ads go into next month's magazines. This letter will clearly state our product's uses, and to dealers its unique profit potential, and how it fits into our present line. They will be told:

1. Size and price range
2. New design features
3. General market need for the heater
4. What it replaces, or how it fits into our line
5. The profit opportunity."

ASSEMBLE USE DATA AND TRADE INFORMATION

The first step of the writer (or product manager) is to assemble, as indicated on the memo, all use-value and trade information on the new product. These then should be written into two sales propositions: 1) uses; 2) profit potential. As set forth elsewhere, the unique or outstanding attribute of the product or service, and its benefit to the reader constitute the letter's proposition. That is its opening.

Anyone who gets a hand into composing a letter should have the memorandum showing the proposition in front of him.

PROCEDURE IN PROJECT-LETTERS

Ideally, when the proposition is composed, it should go to those who will sign the letters with the suggestion that they put it into a letter. Most frequently, the writer proceeds to write the letters, then sends them to the signers. In many companies the president is overburdened and depends on his secretary to reconstruct what he dictates. Or he looks at a piece of paper that seeks an action, tosses it to the secretary and says "tell them no." Or if it is a complaint, the secretary is asked to "get that to soandso and tell him to handle it."

Most secretaries have a great deal to do with their boss' image among his customers. Her well-modulated letters make him sound thoughtful and patient. That is usually favorable, but when the letter involves a selling proposition he should have the proposition in front of him and she should know the original proposition before she attempts to straighten out his dictation. Better yet, on project-letters that go through several hands before they are sent, the original writer's secretary should transcribe exactly as he dictates, good or bad. If the letter is to adhere to its original proposition, only the assigned writer should make changes .

INSERTING PERSONALITY—HOW SHOULD A PRESIDENT SOUND?

A writer who has the assignment to put the final touches on a commercial letter dictated by an executive, to be signed by that officer, has a responsibility that is two-fold. He must check the facts of the proposition, and he determines how far he should go to make it sound like the executive. A corporation head, or marketing director who has a writer on his staff who can insert personality into letters has a fine asset. Letters will reflect a human, warm personality. It is not an easy chore, but it can be learned.

How should a president sound? He should reflect the stereotype of presidents. That means he should sound authoritative. He is not permissive, nor vacillating. When he says something, he expects something to happen. That may not apply to any one president, but "authority" is the key idea to be conveyed to the reader of his letter. A letter from the company president is read with more respectful attention than one from another officer. In turn, other businessmen fully accept the idea that a president is worthy of respect. They also generally agree that the title vice president properly carries considerable weight. In some industries, notably advertising and insurance, the companies kick around v.p. titles in the same way that industrial companies name all monthly salary roll "sales engineers." Yet all have only one president. That may be why being president of any company, large or small, is impressive to those addressed.

A touch to lend personality or authenticity to letters of president status is an occasional possessive reference, such as "my board of directors . . ." or "my people believe. . . ." That form may be boorish or inaccurate, but writers should seek authenticity, and the first person possessive is almost a stereotype.

Top marketing executives will and should write most sales letters that go to customers. An exception might be where the district or branch manager handles sales personally. In cases where companies are not now buying your products, there is little to lose should a company buyer feel slighted when a letter goes to a company officer over his head. If our letter goes from our president to his we can't lose anything. If an officer of our company can establish a management relationship through a letter, that is personality at work in letters.

THE PROPOSITION: ESSENTIAL TO ESTABLISHING PERSONALITY

In examining and emphasizing personality in commercial letters, we must not risk overlooking that the most important element in all commercial letters is the proposition, and right behind that is the absolute need to send it to the right man. That means right man in a company. Before that, we must have researched out the group of names that represents the market we wish to reach. However, until you have a proposition that is worth writing about, it is hardly worthwhile investing in preparations.

While we appear to have agreed on a letter as our form of communications, it might be well to mention that if we are going to send the proposition to a large list, one running into thousands, a printed piece of sales literature will be lower in cost. The only advantage not available in the printed piece is "personality." So we are going ahead with the personalized letter, but we now assume we are paying for the personal factor, and we must be sure to get it.

If your letter looks appropriate to go into the reader president's sanctum with his prime mail, its next strongest quality must be the implication that the writer faces a policy perplexity that he needs some help on. With corporate heads policy perplexities are a compulsion. That's how they got to be president. When he reads your president's letter with its problem, he has met a brother under the skin.

In writing letters reflecting the president's personality the pronoun "I" is not in bad grace. Use it frequently. It somehow is not begrudged by presidents. He may even speak of products or processes as if he held the patents.

REFLECT SENDER'S OCCUPATIONAL INTERESTS

More inherent in our industry are the personality traits reflecting in-company occupations or past skill background. In editing letters to be signed by the president we must be extremely alert to the need for reflecting his occupational interests. Even more, letters written for engineer's signatures must sound engineerish.

Prose style is not of great importance. But regardless of your audience, write in the words that you understand, and use, in your talks to contemporaries. It may be that you are a "long hair" who isn't really understood by anyone. If that is established, don't try to write business letters. By the same token, if you have never mastered grammar don't let your original dictation or writings go to others in a business message. Everyone should not write business letters, just as everyone is not suited interchangeably to every task.

If you are strongly given to the cliché you should have your writings edited. Most advocates of short words and short sentences weaken their message by tiresome repetition of short or pithy sentences or expressions. These often include "colorful" expressions of the type that have been parodied as Madison Avenue jargon. They show themselves frequently in the preemption of athletic expressions. "Hitting the ball;" "team play;" "in left field;"—these and a dozen other tiresome phrases seem to impress those who use them, but they kill interest in what is being said. We shall not devote much time to powerful words and expressions in these notes. If you are addicted to them, cut down gradually. Some day there may be a "Colorful Speaker's Anonymous" but until then each of us should try to speak or write as simply as possible.

EXECUTIVE LEVELS ALWAYS ADDRESS COUNTERPARTS

Our rule of thumb is that executive levels always address counterparts. This is not a hard rule. The important aspect is that our signer be our highest level executive available. Hard rules are difficult to adhere to because of personalities within companies. The president may be rather inarticulate. When he is not highly skilled verbally it is common for department heads to sign letters requiring convincing statements. Of course, in companies employing writers it is immaterial how well any executive writes. Writers must understand their jobs, and they must know company objectives. Even though our president is known throughout the trade as "retiring" his name carries an authority not vested in others.

ELEMENTS IN PERSONALITY BUSINESS LETTERS

When these arrangements are completed, we should begin to consider our content. This should have two major elements requiring attention: 1) the proposition itself and 2) how we shall inject personality, or infiltrate the human reflection that excites empathy. That is: how shall we magnetize our reader toward what we want him to do? The personality in the writing subject is before us, we shall examine it, and when we understand its many forms, we will know more about its effect in commercial letters.

The letter is our only personality technique except the personal call. Far from diminishing the value and need of industrial, technical and business publications to carry your message, the letter program should be planned counterpoint to other media planning.

VALUE OF PERSONALIZED LETTERS IN NEW PRODUCT INTRODUCTIONS

The intrinsic value of writing personalized letters to unfamiliar companies months ahead of our need in introducing a new product is to establish the personality factors. We do not sell the company nor the product. We want the head of that stranger company to know that we are in the industry. We want to edge toward personal acquaintance even though we may later establish a relationship in which our top officers never meet each other.

PLANNING LETTERS IN SERIES

One value of planning letters in series is that we can stake out some material for later letters when we start our first letter. The first letter will have in its opening the identification of our type of company. That definitive material will be repeated in each letter. If we are a company well-known in the industry, the identification is confined to the product, service or division that is new. Our company or product identification should not imply that the audience does not know it. Nor should it be separated from the narrative. Example:

> As a specialized producer of industrial ——————— serving the industry for many years, I am taking the liberty of writing to several industry leaders whose requirements may coincide with an engineering development we have in process. Unlike our long-established line of ——————— that are confined to a few industry users, the products under development will reach for applications among a majority of the principal companies in our industry. In view of that, I am asking if your policies would permit your people to disclose to our operations manager some facts related to your volume requirements.

The specific request should be one that could logically receive either a "yes" or "no" answer. Our purpose in writing is to get our letterhead and our president's name into the hands of the president of that unfamiliar company. We have told him who we are in a way that implies we are known in the industry.

The personality factors in the above are two-fold: our president is asking his counterpart's aid and advice, and we are adhering closely to the kinship of our industry.

Situations such as indicated here are extremely well-suited to the unique value of personalized letters conveying personality and human factors. Simply addressing that president by name and our president's signature at the end of the letter is business personality. However, the "fellow industry member" is our strong point in the example shown.

EFFECTIVE WRITTEN IDEAS DEPEND ON WORD PERSONALITY

Personality factors in business letters may be entirely mechanical. Kinship may be established by the salutation "Dear Fellow Member" of any group from a bowling club to a periodic book-mailing club. When we consider words or terms as factors to establish personality or individuality we come across almost as many words that are taboo as words that are acceptable. Letters are not essentially dependent upon grammar or rhetoric, but the effectiveness of written ideas depends heavily upon the words portraying or describing them.

In the discussion to follow we deal largely with rhetoric and ways of thinking about our recipients. The starting point will be our proposition start. Do not supply the background. If it is a fire sale, describe the merchandise affected in one term, such as smoke-damaged, undamaged, etc. If it is a consumer letter addressed "Dear Customer" do not include in your proposition that it is only for customers. Do not say "once in a lifetime." Give the is and was prices if it is a real bargain.

These are a taste of letter-rhetoric. We will examine a dozen or so such taboos—often merely trite—that always diminish the letter's impact and the reader's favorable image of you.

CHAPTER XI

THE LETTER TO THE EMPLOYEES

Consumer and commercial letters are planned to create a situation, employee letters are planned to meet an existing one. A first consideration for business letters is selecting a market or audience; for the employee letter we already have our audience. After we agree on these differences, most other aspects of the two letters have great similarity.

Practically all companies have employees' communications programs. Regardless of other ramifications, letters to the home are usually a part of it, even if confined to the annual Christmas greetings. Well-planned employee letter programs should bring five or six letters during the year. If we analyzed all situations where home letters are used, we would find that a majority have a defensive motivation. The best letter programs have as their mood, "So that you may be fully informed. . . ."

COVERING TOUCHY RELATIONSHIPS AND TELLING THE COMPANY STORY

The dramatic outside encroachments upon employee attitudes are the always-increasing governmental and labor union involvements. Except for "exempt"—those on the monthly roll-letters even inferentially touching those relationships must walk a tightrope, legally and ethically. Much more to the point are letters telling the company story: security, opportunity, philosophy, aimed at reducing simple attrition and the related costs of training new people. Unlike the misfired business letter that lands in the wastebasket, the misfired employee letter can land on the bulletin board at the union hall—often deservedly. Poorly conceived and timed business letters lose sales. The damage can be much more serious from misconceived employee letters.

THE SITUATION DETERMINES THE SIGNATURE

In larger companies, employee communications generally originate with the personnel administrator. Their context and reasons for writing determine whose signatures they carry. Half of them may come from administrative officers who handle employee affairs; the other half, or more, from the president, plant manager, or a divisional head in plant cities. Unless they involve situations that have already attracted outside notice and require policy definition, the plant manager usually should sign them. If the press already has noticed the situation, unless it involves a technical employee relation matter, the top officer in the plant city involved should speak for the company. The personnel officer signs letters discussing "relationships" or routine announcements that could have community interest. Letters during controversies are never routine, and must be approached cautiously.

In employee communications, it may be said that sometimes the letter that is not sent is more important than the one that is. This is one reason for pre-determining how many letters to send, and then adhering to that total. Letters sent to union-represented employees on matters that the union has become involved in are high on the list of those that should not be sent. There are exceptions.

EMPLOYEE LETTERS ARE OFTEN DEFENSIVE

Elementally, employee letters are often defensive. A reason for this is that many companies characteristically avoid subjects related to improved worker climate. Companies sending letters to all employees are not always free to discuss matters otherwise related to union contracts. It is important that a "shot from the hip" letter does not damage the administration of these agreements. Letters to the homes of union employees are definitely considered unfriendly by elected union officers. This explains why some companies seldom use letters. It is a reason for double care in what you say and when you say it. We have said, be very thoughtful in employee letters. We will add, use them steadily if you want your story told, and have them signed by the top man.

LETTERS WHERE UNIONS EXIST

The company should always send letters to the employees' homes during times when they are considering voting on the question of union representation. Where it is a question of union or not, the company should concede nothing. This suggests further discussion of the limitations of letters.

Employee letters as such should not attempt to do a conclusive job. At best, where any employee crisis is involved, they state the case that must be implemented by the supervisors or foremen. Letters are relatively weakest in times of crisis. At those times, the good supervisor is your salvation. But if you can say something to strengthen him, a letter to the employee home is frequently the best way to do it. Such letters quickly become union targets. And they get to the newspapers fast.

In assuming that all companies have some occasion to write letters to employees' homes, we should further assume that they have two communications programs: one to salary employees and another to all employees. Unless the matter is technical, companies have no occasion to write to hourly people alone, excluding the salary roll.

Management seldom is able to realize the inherent nature of communications between union and employee, or between an employee organizing an office union and his fellows. The long years of close and personal relationships between the company and employees fade shockingly fast when security is questioned. By their nature, unions are communications vehicles. Elected officers understand their constituencies well. Strong unions got that way through communications that operated in an extremely sympathetic climate. Unions are in trouble whenever they want something from the company that the membership is not "demanding."

A LETTERS PROGRAM SHOWS MANAGEMENT'S INTEREST

Considerable emphasis is given the above fundamentals because it is not possible to plan employee letters without being aware of the values of employee influences. This is a reason for suggesting a program to send five or six letters annually. Just as the employees' publication should have space where the management always has voice, so should management establish, in times of quiet, methods such as letters to the homes by which management speaks to employees.

Taken from the viewpoint of improving climate and giving management a chance to show that its interest is with the people, employee letters should embrace some "visiting."

In the commercial letter we do not visit because it is an imposition on time that the reader cannot afford. In employee letters, time is no problem. As we shall discuss, he may not read it at all, but whoever is the best reader in the family, often mama, reads it carefully.

If management has illusions that letters or any communications direct from it can supplant supervisor influence, or any matter that belongs on the bargaining table, it had best forget letters before it starts. The reason they work well, if everything is done properly, is that they augment the supervisor. The unions have fantastic communications potentials. Every time a stenographer is reprimanded, or a mail boy laid off, someone mentions the office union in the plant across town.

We can generalize that a formal supervisory communications program must always precede employee communications from management. This may involve letters, although the nature of this relationship suggests bulletins and meetings should follow a schedule regardless of in-plant conditions. Supervisors either come from the ranks or their closeness to rank and file give them a chance to feel employee attitudes. Yet, their very closeness puts them in the position of the Army sergeant who knows all the gripes.

LETTER OPPORTUNITIES: RUMORS, FALSE REPORTS, JOB CHANGES

Letters to employees are suggested by reports of rumors and false statements in the plant or by uneasiness in the offices when improvements require job changes. Change is the union's best friend. But unions characteristically pose the questions to make the company the competition. They knock company motives more aggressively than competitors knock company products. So whether we have union representation or not, all letters to employees should be written as if an organizer were going to answer them.

PLANNING LETTERS TO ESTABLISH ACCEPTANCE

Our discussion of the employee letter is being retarded to bring us abreast as to considerations that must precede writing. Commercial letters should be planned in series to establish acceptance against need. Company should always write to all salary people before telling anyone else, whenever modernized equipment will cause changes. But after an order for data processing machinery is placed, it is very late to tell office people. They knew about it before the executive committee okayed the purchase. The letters, dwelling on competitive aspects of modernization, should be planned.

Communications with employees should not differ greatly whether a union is involved or not. Even companies that have never had a union, and especially an office union, must know that they are meeting and surpassing union benefits. The union's message to everyone's employee appears in newspapers, or on radio and TV, and in barroom conversation every day. Management's messages have very few such "windfall" opportunities. Unions employ some well-educated people.

They have these well-educated people write material and speak out for them. But at the local level, their letters to the membership for organizational purposes are characteristically extremely weak and unsophisticated. The only less effective letters common to industry are those sometimes "fired" by the boss when he is mad or those in which the company appeals to patriotism. Both union letters and badly conceived company letters invariably employ good grammatic construction. In employee letters, this is more important than in commercial letters.

A commercial letter lives or dies on the judgment of its proposition. The employee letter has several lives. If it goes to an office employee at home, she tosses it to her husband or to her mother after reading it. If they are sitting down to eat, the letter is discussed. A reason that the grammar must be watched is that secondary readers watch it.

TIMING: NERVE CENTER OF EMPLOYEE LETTERS

Timing is the nerve center of employee letters. Here is why it is more important than in other letters. These letters are defensive, in a technical sense. Fighting from the defensive stance is difficult. Therefore, we should anticipate situations (as indicated for data processing) so that we are not "answering charges."

Letters seldom can be used once negotiations are at the bargaining table. On the other hand, information on economic climate and company progress should go to employees well ahead of bargaining time. If we have a ninety-day cycle established (loosely followed) we have occasion to keep our people aware that competition is watching us.

Employee administrators for larger companies where management is professionally enlightened as to techniques, are painfully aware of management's sincerity in viewing union objectives as nefarious. Management that does not deal directly with labor reads what the unions are telling the people, calculates that it's "pretty dumb stuff," and concludes that what the employees need to know are the "facts of life." The problem is that is exactly what the union has told people, and it is why the union has their ear.

We have said that an employee letter should pay considerable attention to rhetoric, but that we need not be so greatly concerned with "construction." Just as employees are a captive audience for the union, they are for the company. One difference is that the emotions involved are different. Employees compulsively think the company has an axe to grind. Union messages frequently come to them from "old pals in the office," and disarm.

SECONDARY READERS: MAJOR TARGET OF EMPLOYEE LETTERS

Our letter should be not only our best writing, it must make a lot of sense to mama or to the married woman employee's husband. The secondary reader is a major target of any letter from the company. A letter may be said to be wasted when the writer fails to properly gauge the feelings of the employees. It is worse than wasted if it "talks down" to them. Executives who envisage the employees as a faceless group will very often estimate that anything longer than a paragraph, with words of more than two syllables, will not be read by employees. That may be true. Perhaps nothing beyond sports results or comic strips are read by them. But every family has a reader. He or she is the one to write the letter to. He can read well and his opinion is respected at home. He may be the one they are sending to college.

LETTERS TO SALARIED AND HOURLY WORKERS

We shall start discussions of how you proceed to write by listing our audiences, in their order, as potential audiences for letters:

        1. Salary people
        2. All employees
        3. Hourly roll

Salary groups are divided into clerical and "exempt"—supervisory and high-grade jobs. Immediately we shall not think of the group from sales executives and supervisors to top management as a letter audience, except as they figure as salary people. Rather than suggest "hourly roll" as an audience, it is more practical to plan to send letters aimed at them to "all employees." We have listed the hourly roll, but it should be used as such only infrequently. The practical division is actually two—salary and all employees.

Before we undertake analysis of an opening for a letter, we should briefly discuss our sources for letter materials. In commercial letters we adhere closely to the inherent proposition. In those we described our product or service and told how it can increase profit for the recipient. Then we go into the body of the letter to tell how and why. That formula is necessary because we are racing the clock. Our reader does not have time for any delays.

LETTERS TO ANNOUNCE CHANGES

The employee at home is differently situated. Time is no factor, so we can improve the climate before we mention why we are really writing. We must assume that the employee wonders why you are writing to him. He may be suspicious, or at least wary. It is almost impossible to compose a letter involving company attitudes that jumps into the subject. The degree of urgency regulates the nature of the letter opening. For example, if the letter's purpose is to "announce" a new tape-control machine in the shop, or automatic machines taking over office functions, the lead-time is very important. Generally, mention of the subject related to office workers should be started as soon as you know you are going ahead with the installations. Where the changes involve hourly people, generally it is better to wait until the machines are delivered, installed and in preparation for operation.

In both of the above cases, the first mention should not be the "subject" of the letter. For example: if automatic equipment is being installed in the shop and a company-wide vacation is scheduled before it goes into operation, the "subject" of the letter should be the vacation, and the machines would come into it in a manner such as, ". . . during the shut-down we expect further progress in the placement of new tape-control units. With cost reductions these promise, our intention is to go after some business that we missed earlier to a lower bidder."

Where office automation is planned, the keys to understanding are "growth and capabilities," with an office-wide "training program." Nowadays offices are expected to become automated, but employees whose service pre-dates electronics resist its advances either visibly or otherwise. Management should have day-to-day programs to fully inform on this subject because it frequently is greatly feared by salary people, even those whose jobs are not affected. The total employee attitude is seldom visible to management at the outset because new equipment shrinks the employee rolls. There is no help shortage then. Displaced persons have no immediate recourse and others sit quietly until the changes are made. Negative attitudes do not surface at once, but they are a by-product of cost programs that can cost money a year or two later.

LETTERS TO EMPLOYEES BEING "LAID OFF"

Perhaps the most difficult letter to write is that to employees who are being laid off. It is especially difficult when you know that there is little likelihood that they will be re-employed.

Let us suppose that our company is subject to seasonal operating cut-backs that cause office and hourly lay-offs. We should consider two letters at the time they take their severance: one to those laid off and another to those not laid off. The letter to the lay-offs could start:

> "Because of the seasonal nature of our business, our constant planning objective is to reduce work-loads at our peak periods and sustain higher operations rates when the seasonal demands slacken as they have now. We have made progress, but as yet we have not overcome the industry pattern it reflects. It is costly to us and even more serious for many of our employees. We regret that this is the cause of interruption to your service.
>
> "As in other years, we hopefully look forward to the return to higher operating rates. However, in fairness to you, we suggest that you feel free to seek and take on employment elsewhere. It is not possible to accurately forecast our needs, either as to the timing or which operations will be involved. As in the past, we shall continue to seek improvement in our market levels, but we do not want to ask you to wait.
>
> "If our personnel department can be of service in your moves toward other employment, we want you to know that they will welcome the opportunity."

LETTERS TO EASE FEAR OF WORKERS NOT "LAID OFF"

The reason those not laid-off should have a letter is that until they are told otherwise, they fear being next. Example:

> "As you know, the seasonal nature of our business makes necessary reductions in our force at this season. Those whose services could best be spared have been notified. To the others we can only say that we are gratified that it appears we will go through this season with no further changes.
>
> "As much as we regret the difficulties faced by those whose employment is interrupted, it is even more in keeping with our responsibilities that the company's operations be sound. In our decision to continue at the new operating rate we calculated that we could count on the fullest cooperation from those whose function was not interrupted. We are aware that an especially heavy burden falls on all employees. Competitive conditions have been somewhat more severe than in recent years.

"We believe that we can hold our own against further inroads by competition. Because we face some increased costs for materials and other essentials in the months ahead, we see some rough going. Our best weapon in this competitive battle is the loyalty and dedication of our people. None of us would choose to operate within the limitations we now face. We have tightened our belts and become a lean, hard organization. We are geared to meet our cost objectives, but realizing these goals will require the best moral effort that each of us can put into it. I am sure we can all count on each one doing his share in this stern assignment."

These are both "visiting letters." The one for employees laid off makes clear that this is not a "temporary" lay-off. Sometimes supervisors (who are always the ones to give the original notification to the people) leave an impression that an employee will be automatically reinstated. Evidence is complete that any employee who is cut-back will come back if he cannot do better, and if he can do better, he will not even talk to his former employer. Letters of termination should not commit to re-hire, unless you know you will want them in a tight labor market.

WRITING EMPLOYEES AT HOME

The classic "letter to the employees at home" that has dominated the employee communications field in past years has been the type that attacks the union's demands or petition to represent. Management has a good success record here. Where they have failed is mainly where their viewpoint was overly emotional. Unions are frequently vulnerable when the membership loses its militancy. Letters telling of possible deterioration of the competitive position of Hometown if costs increase, cause the wives to worry about a plant withdrawal. Such implications or statements can be made only if the plant can leave town. If it is not ready to go if the "rumor" fails, it is far better that the idea never be inserted. Once insecurity gains headway, the path to further unionization is smoothed.

OFFSETTING EMPLOYEE FEARS

Relationships between the company and its certified unions take on as many patterns as between two persons. Some live stormy lives together between contract renewals, but seem reconciled and re-negotiate without great cost. Others appear to be aware of common interests but create havoc at each contract renewal time. Because the union's function includes uninterrupted communications with the employees, the company should have a program by which it makes its position known on matters affecting security. Employees' characteristic sense of insecurity is often the basis for the strongest hold the union has and company planning is often damaged most by rumors or premature stories of coming changes.

Unless plans for plant removal are underway, it is the company's responsibility to allay apprehensions of the "plant leaving town." In some high-cost areas, management has mistakenly used that threat in seeking cost reductions or to offset new union demands. Letters should be used to remove such fears if the company hopes to gain employee cooperation. Uncertainties regarding the future are a part of man's make-up that unions have found very useful. Unless this is kept in mind coninuously, management is baited into playing the union's game.

USING COMPETITION TO CREATE BETTER OFFICE MORALE

Competition is the strongest weapon to suggest to employees that they do a good job. That may be from a fellow employee in the office or shop or it may be the competitive attractiveness of products from another company or the fear of "cheap labor" imports. But management does not need to use competition as a club. The employee never forgets his insecurity. It drives him to seeking a hiding place—the union.

Suppose our aim is to plan four or five letters to go to all employees during the next 12 months to create a better climate that will reflect in fewer grievances and better office morale.

We shall use "competition" in a constructive way. Such letters may have any arrangement that you wish as far as readership is concerned. They may be identified as "one of a series" or as "our policy of writing when we have something to say affecting our employees." Should that vein be followed, an opening for the first letter could be:

"The country and our industry are undergoing changes that

all of us might better understand. Most of us are inclined to jump to conclusions that we later may regret. Earlier this year our market studies reflected that prices would soften as supplies increased. That is essentially what has occurred. It does not mean necessarily that the market is over-produced. To achieve competitive volume and keep our goods in free supply we must ship until buying rates are outpaced. Full supplies are normal for our industry and most others. There is nothing alarming in that condition: it is one we fight in the market place with some success.

"That summary represents our outlook and it is the outlook of our competition. Obviously it is not a climate that any of us would test by any price increases. At least our company would not gamble that way. But we do have some cost increases over which we have little control. We are managing to avoid other increases by unqualified resistance. Any supplier whose prices increase risks losing our business. Within the company we have made excellent progress with our cost-reduction program. The determination of all departments to hold the line is showing results.

"We are continuing our studies toward new products suited to changes in our customers' needs. Our success in breaking into new fields will hinge on having competitive costs.

"We shall continue our methods studies toward that end . . . ."

The purpose of this example is to indicate two things: 1) Employee letters should not try to be elemental. Employees who can't understand them or read them will get the message from someone at home, or from an employee who does read. 2) Your letter need not be short, nor loaded with simple examples. The readers have plenty of time. They read sports pages by the hour. Our only word of caution is: do not send too many letters and do not use the subjunctive or other connotations of uncertainty. Avoid "so you see, if we can do this our outlook is good." Avoid making comparisons of the company's performance in one city vs. another city.

In letters that follow the first, the opening reference should be, ". . . in our policy of keeping you informed. . . ."

This type of letter is actually your counter-balance to the union. It should be so sound that when it is analyzed at the union planning council there can be no rebuttal. Always introduce your subject by reflecting recent returns from the market place.

Because letters of this type come from skilled communicators in employee relations, our aim here is mainly to suggest that these letters preferably run for two pages. That is not a theory of communications. It is a fact that two pages, written to employees on almost any subject, is more effective than one page. In lining up your proposition, divide your materials into two segments: those of general information nature and those having a direct bearing on the in-plant situation. In the general category you may mention as many elements as you wish. When speaking of affairs in the offices or plant, confine the topics of your discussion to not more than two and preferably one topic.

LETTERS TO SALARY PEOPLE

The potential of the letter to employees on the salary rolls is immeasurably greater than the one to hourly people regardless of union relationships. What is termed "productivity" in the plants is regulated by many things. Its parallel in the offices is "morale," and when it reflects negatively, the company loses a great deal of what it can gain by modern methods.

Letters to salary people have a dimension not present in the type discussed above. Most salary people can be classified as either "administrative," or potentially advanceable. The others are the "exempt" qualified as management. The great bulk of salary employees in medium and large companies are those overtime potentials whose functions are close to supervision and higher management. Even though many of them are cynical, the fact that they went into "white-collar" work indicates some interest in either advancement or personal status.

Said one other way, salary people tend to want "climate" instead of the "conditions" wanted by hourly employees. Their sense of insecurity is equal. Salary people appear to have more security, but it is offset by their greater sensitivity. In one or another of its forms, electronic data processing systems are the best identified threat to office people. Regardless of the degree of automation, even its operators seldom recover their full sense of security. This aspect of the business is a reason for management doing more than conducting "training" or discussing in the company employees' magazine. Even the fully-mechanized office company should not permit its employees to go long without hearing the company outlook. It may not come immediately, but just as unions took over neglected industrial workers, these employees will be easy for organizers unless they feel close to management.

RESIST PUBLICIZING AUTOMATED EQUIPMENT

Companies should resist publicizing automatic equipment. That may be advantageous to shareholders, customers and company officers, but it worries neighborhood families, younger employees, and most of those employed for other than control machine positions. There is no head-to-head argument supporting modernization effectively with younger salary people. They live in a society where non-organizational life prevails. Their neighbors are concerned that "machines will replace men." Companies should play down the place of automation in office control. The publicity of giant producers of "machines with memories and brains" has created a situation that has caused some companies to abandon morale-building programs. The facts are that sharper efforts should be made to offset the negative situation.

Mention of that situation to some "electronic experts" may bring the answer that "everyone knows automation is here; you can't stop progress." That is true. All people are not being replaced, but individual companies must reduce their rolls. Some must go. The most important letters to employees may very well be those explaining the company's training program to offset skill modifications related to modernization. As indicated earlier, change of any kind is a scare-idea to employees. Security is the strong term. This is what is most wanted by lower salary groups. Management's strongest term in communications is "competition." Lay-offs must be linked to competition. At Detroit, highly automated tooling installed at costs of millions of dollars has sustained high level car production even while tens of thousands are laid off. This has been a long-running serial labeled, "Technological Improvement."

INDUSTRIAL RELATIONS FOR GOOD COMMUNICATIONS

The auto industry has a very responsible attitude toward this type of reduction in employment. Its industrial relations programs are numerous, and its labor contracts face up to the situation. Some smaller industries, retailers, and most service industries have not always adopted the long view toward employee dislocations. Our interest is in individual companies, not in companies as groups. We know that good communications sometimes perform greater changes than operational activities. From the very earliest thoughts of electronic machinery in offices, the company should begin telling its employees about it. Away back in the early 1930's the American Telephone and Telegraph Company began telling its employees and the public that the new automatic equipment would *increase* jobs. And it was said so often that other businessmen began quoting it in their speeches. That is the type of "communications" we recommend, and anytime is still not too late to tell employees that the company has an interest in their futures.

GOOD SITUATIONS FOR EMPLOYEE LETTERS

The two elements or situations that properly suggest communicating with employees are 1) the existence of plans and activities on the part of others speaking to them with reference to their employment and 2) changes within the company, especially when these changes are related to cost reduction.

Situation number one is generally related to union activities. The second one is related to things we do that give cause for anxieties about the future.

In posing examples for each of these letters, the aim has been to illustrate the need for man-to-man talking. At the risk of being "not read or understood" these letters fully explain some complex situation the company faces. They reflect great interest in having employees understand company problems. And they do not attack anyone.

CHAPTER XII

LETTERS TO STOCKHOLDERS

The wide diffusion of stock ownership since the early 1930's greatly influenced growing opinion among management that it is worthwhile to volunteer information to shareholders. Similarly to the wisdom of "keeping employees informed," telling owners more about the business and its objectives can be a useful management tool. But volunteering information to owners has some limitations.

Stockholder communications are not aimed at identifiable individuals with whom we have personal dealings. The highly publicized aspects of corporate life including the owners who are "widows and children," the avaricious lawyer who organizes a "raid" and the heckler who comes to the annual meeting do not in themselves justify management planning of volunteer information. Under regulations and laws, companies supply basic information if their shares are traded. Owners come into possession on the basis of that information. Publicly-owned companies must report annually. A great many do so quarterly. There is no moral reason for volunteer or additional stockholder information.

PRESENTING A "GROWTH" IMAGE

Stockholders have many ways of learning about the company. The concensus of their appraisal of performance and outlook is reflected in the stock's trading price. Profits are what interest shareholders. But partially because of tax considerations, many investors prefer "growth." An obvious conclusion is that well-managed companies earn profits and present a "growth image."

That modest-sounding conclusion as to management's attitude toward shareholder opinion may have in it the strongest reason for considering a corporate policy involving writing letters to stockholders several times annually. Growth either comes from within through product development or market expansion or it comes through acquisitions and mergers. The latter type is much faster and in almost every instance it is the more sure road. Excluding the largest corporations which have departments and other means of planning growth in all its forms, every company with an active acquisition interest should have some degree of a volunteer stockholder communications program. Letters are by far the best means management has to speak directly.

ACQUISITION SITUATIONS

Characteristically, in acquisition situations the larger company is the acquirer, the survivor. In addition to being larger, its shares are almost always publicly traded. The most frequent reason for smaller companies being available is their need of capital. As the "bride," the acquired does the selecting. Among several suitors offering resources, diversification and management, they select the one felt to offer the best stockholder relationship for them and their families.

ESTABLISH A FREQUENCY PATTERN
FOR STOCKHOLDER LETTERS

This summarizes the best reason for volunteer information to stockholders planning for medium and smaller size companies. The largest companies almost without exception have programs. Once a company is committed to a "letters to the stockholders" program, it must follow whatever frequency pattern it starts with. Erratic timing of letters can arouse suspicion and regulatory agencies frown. The most widely practiced timing is quarterly. This coincides with the established reporting practices of most security exchanges.

A VIEWPOINT PHILOSOPHY: A RECURRING THEME LINE

As indicated earlier, the stockholder is not a "captive" in the sense that an employee is. The company is not characteristically on the defensive with them. Even when management is not reporting satisfactory earnings, it need not be on the defensive. The defensive is bad in all business relationships. Letters to stockholders should be based on a viewpoint philosophy. That is to say, they should have a recurring theme line that will become familiar to recipients. For example: ". . . in keeping with our aim to point out the significant events bearing on our business during each period. . . ."

CHIEF EXECUTIVE SIGNATURES TO INDICATE PERSONAL INTEREST

The responsibility for stockholder communications is in the financial department. But the chief executive officer signs communications. Where that title is not used, and in some instances, two officers sign. An advantage of a single signature is the indication of "personal interest."

Relatively few companies, and these are confined to the larger ones, have investor stockholders such as institutions, foundations and funds and insurance companies. These professional owners are interested equally with small owners. And because they study operations consistently they can smell unrealistic information. All stockholder letters should be written as though they were going to these professionals.

TECHNIQUES IN PLANNING STOCKHOLDER LETTERS

In proceeding to examine how we should assemble information as we would a proposition in a sales letter, we shall consider that a letter will go to stockholders quarterly. The necessity for a viewpoint that suggests a theme must be a part of our original decision to write to stockholders. Assuming that almost every company has some interest in acquisitions, we shall examine techniques with that as our long-range objective. If we write good, sensible letters we know stockholders will welcome them. But, we must be ready and able to do more than reflect that we think it is good business to have our stockholders well-informed. We must keep in mind that our shareholders are readers of the financial press. They may frequently read comprehensive stories about our industry. Our letters must not seem to overlook how events in the news effect us. Even more, we should be most careful to review market and product status before we make final the "proposition" of our letter.

STEPS IN CONSTRUCTING STOCKHOLDER LETTERS

While the financial department should have responsibility for letter content, the assembled facts should be written by a writer more likely identified as public relations. Good financial executives seldom embellish sufficiently to compose voluntary stockholder information. After a writer constructs the letter, it should go to the chief executive officer. Here we come to the most critical phase of handling programs of this type.

The chief executive officer should read what has been written, knowing that it is based on financial department facts and composed by a public relations writer who may also be an advertising or publicity man. Then the chief officer should re-write or dictate his version. That is an almost necessary technique if the letters are to be worthwhile. The real value of using letters rather than printed matter, or in writing at all, is to create a bond between management and owners. What the chief officer puts down should be substantially what is sent. It might be useful to send the rewritten letter back to financial for checking. Also, it may want a little polishing by the writer who composed it. Unlike commercial letters, these should be rhetorically impeccable, with this one reservation: if the chief officer has any recognizable speech mannerisms, do not delete them. They help establish the theme line related to cumulative effect. Also, writers should be careful not to distort emphasis of what chief executives say.

Mature public relations writers train their ears to reflect the thinking and expression of those they serve. It is not often that those businessmen sound like young graduates of a business school. But that is what many "prepared" letters from chief executives resemble.

Persons trained in writing contracts and other formal documents must be extremely versatile to write effective informal employee or stockholder communications. Labor and financial writings must be accurate as to fact, but they will not do what is expected unless they establish the right image of the signer.

WELCOMING NEW STOCKHOLDERS

There is no rule that says a company must acknowledge the presence of a new stockholder. Most companies do not. But it creates a fine impression to wave a "howdy" to an investing owner. In actively traded stocks some holders are highly transient, but some of this turnover habit could be slowed if an owner were welcomed aboard. This type of letter should be pre-written completely. To the new owner, "being wanted" is our intent.

AVOID ADVANCE INFORMATION DISCLOSURES

In some types of business letters a strategic opening is the type that says, ". . . prior to our releasing to the press, we want you to know that . . . ." Avoid all such opening statements in stockholders' letters. Regardless of security exchange and other regulations, never communicate any financial fact regarding your company as "advance" or special information. Except for the welcome aboard letters and similar socially-motivated messages stockholder letters should be addressed: *To All Stockholders*.

    To re-emphasize this point: almost any form of communication with owners or others is subject to regulation for the protection of all concerned. It is secondary whether you are violating a regulation. Make it your communications rule to include in stockholders' letters only matters that could be put into a news release.

    Do not write or send a letter to stockholders disclosing operating information prior to a stockholders' meeting. If such information is essential at that time, it should be in the proxy statement. It might be mentioned here: do not send financially-related information to anyone including employees prior to a stockholders' meeting.

ECONOMIC FORECASTS—BEST LEFT TO MEETINGS AND REPORTS

The foregoing does not in any sense restrain the company officers from statements between quarterly reports expressing an outlook or predicting or forecasting results. Such officials are on their own as to benefits. There is no rule against forecasting outlook to stockholders. It is suggested that such "forecasts" be confined to meetings, annual and quarterly reports and other occasions where the subject is at hand.

TREAT STOCKHOLDERS AS OWNERS

In many types of communications it is desirable to anticipate negative situations and communicate with interested parties. This is frequently recommended in employee letters and when used properly is useful in commercial letters. It is difficult to estimate how it can be useful as financial forecasting in letters written to stockholders. Technically, stockholders are captives. They can cease being so on no notice, as can an employee or dealer. But during the stockholder's tenure as an owner, he should be treated as one. Technically, to the stockholder, the company is "your company." Some reference in that vein should be in the letter. Overdoing it is similar to adding the appendage "sir" when you address him. It's nice, but not too much.

PADDING THE LETTER'S BODY AND CLOSE

In commercial letters we aim at directness. In stockholders' letters a small helping of mumbo-jumbo is often useful. Specifically, your stockholder may have only that aspect of his life in common with any other stockholder. He may be a giant investment trust, a large insurance company, widow (the most famed category), bank, other corporation or a business man. The type of stockholder who may get the most effective information from your letter is very likely to be the professional investor. By the same token, he may get all he wants to know out of one sentence. In fact there may be only one, or at most three, "working sentences" in your letter. But it may be a basic problem in stockholder letters that you may not write a one-two-three-sentence letter to them. Just as they would feel cheated with a three-sentence sermon on Sunday, they want a longer letter once it gets to them. Rather than attempting to disclose pertinent matters that are not directly aimed at better understanding of questions "in the news" your best procedure is to pad out the body and close of the letter with semantic exercises of a highly subjunctive nature.

As a further word to establish the necessity of the foregoing, let us look at a "financial trend bulletin." A majority of these subscriber letters serve a useful function to their recipients. At prices ranging from $25 to $100 and more, they are renewed on a ratio similar to that of more obvious information sources. We have no intent to minimize or even to categorically discuss them. But by their nature they convey a great amount of subjunctive mumbo-jumbo. This mood of communications is especially suited to stockholder information because it takes the place of something that should not be imparted.

CONFINE LETTERS TO PERTINENT MATTERS

Stockholders' letters should confine their working information to one, two, but not more than three matters of pertinence. This does not include matters on the balance sheet. Upon some occasions the entire letter may be a point by point commentary on the balance sheet. This practice is not recommended for any but the most sophisticated financial communications specialist. It can be helpful and enlightening to illuminate some facets of an operations sheet, but management is asking for trouble if it periodically opens up questions regarding running a competitive company.

Earlier in the pros and cons of business letters, we discussed specific operating aspects. There are contingencies in the life of every company when it is greatly to its advantage to have established a habit of communications with its owners. These times include when dissident stockholders or other questioners come on the horizon. Most financial officers in companies are fairly sensitive to movements (unusual buying or selling) of their stock. Sometimes "invasions" or acquisition intent can be sensed in these moves. On other occasions they may reflect unfavorable industry situations, such as impending negative legislation or a revolutionary product or process in the offing that may obsolete your entire line.

A basic rule of communications is that it is advantageous to have an established medium when you want a message carried. This is most obvious in the acceptance of the national financial daily edition. But even though a financial publication owned your stock, you cannot frequently insert "pertinent" information there to reach your stockholders. The "frequently" is employed because some companies do exactly that. Our question is related to stockholder information confined to them. If you initiate a letter program now and continue it for the next 12 months, you will have an excellent medium from then on for whatever is legal and advisable to tell them. Specifically, if a group is quietly buying your stock with a threat that it may come into the open and offer tenders, you should tell the stockholders.

HANDLING DEFENSIVE SITUATIONS

Sometimes outsiders buy a stock with the intent to gain a voice through their holdings. If that is undesirable, management's responsibility is to analyze why outsiders see the situation as accessible. If the stock is undervalued, a letter program is not necessarily the basic tool to combat the invader. We must assume that management makes other moves to dislocate the "bargain" aspect of the company's shares. Then whether or not you have established a letter program, a letter to stockholders is almost mandatory. It should go as quickly as management has aligned its "ducks in a row" even though it is only two weeks ahead of the annual meeting.

The stockholder letter related to a defensive situation is very similar to the employee letter. Potentially you have an adversary who is depreciating your reputation. The most important starting point is to have all facts related to his interest in front of you. Frequently well-managed companies permit too much cash to show. This will attract an invader who might want to come into possession of it for (legal) purposes of investing in, or shoring up, another company.

MERGER OPPORTUNITIES: SPELL OUT THE FACTS

Where cases similar to the above are involved, they should be spelled out to all stockholders as carefully as if they were all old widows.

More common among smaller publicly-held companies are situations where a legitimate merger opportunity is sensed by management. This cannot be told immediately either to stockholders or others. Where our company would be the expendable member, the need for our enjoying a good degree of confidence would be obvious. No matter how fairly and properly the ratios are established to determine a trading base, some shareholders will feel that a better price should be offered for their holdings. Professional investors seldom activate an objection or join others who object. The objector is more frequently a professional or businessman. He is at a disadvantage in that he does not have the names of the stockholders. But he may have an advantage if you do not use the list to communicate.

THE STOCKHOLDERS RELATIONS ASPECT OF PUBLIC RELATIONS

Our aim here is not to depart from our purpose of discussing letters. However, when your company is in an unfavorable situation regarding outsiders buying in or any situation involving an acquisition or merger, the subject is literally, "Stockholders Relations aspect of Public Relations." If your company has public relations counsel, he should be on these situations from the outset.

For example, when an outsider attempts to purchase your company's stock for purposes of becoming an elected member of the board, his ethics are subject to question. Even when an "outsider" comes to or writes to the management and discloses his intentions, from the management's (your employer) viewpoint, he is an intruder and unwanted. Unless there are unusual elements that are known to your management, you should put an agent to work investigating everything possible regarding the activities and background of the outsider. He may have a history of getting into companies that did not thereafter thrive. If you find negative aspects in his past, you have the biggest gun in the business arsenal. This is your armament for a stockholder letter. Never write anything on the defensive if you have a choice of positions. Of course, in taking the offensive, you must adhere closely to legal advice.

Should your company be initiating a stockholder letter program and it already has such devices as a dramatized annual meeting with box lunches and other gimmicks, it is advisable that some of the present activities be eliminated. While keeping stockholders informed is one thing, we must evalute the stockholders who physically participate in the meeting. Corporate giants are doing a fine job of showing their interest in holders with big room, big city meetings. Smaller companies are asking for new problems if they increase their attentions to their stockholders. It must be borne in mind that good information, on the most convenient frequency basis, is what is most valuable to management and to holders.

CHAPTER XIII

DEPARTMENT STORE PERSONALIZED LETTERS

Note: Enclosures vs. Letters

Bill enclosures are so effectively established that most large stores sending monthly bills to their customers figure that they have the "mail front" pretty well saturated. An informal inquiry among some two hundred women charge customers of six large stores in a city of 100,000 population disclosed that not one of these women objected to bill enclosures. Because most advertising mail has some objectors, the acceptance for bill enclosures may be unique.

While none of these women objected to bill enclosures, slightly more than half answered "No" to the question, "Do you recall ever going to buy or ordering an item offered in a folder with your monthly bill?" However, other questions established the value of enclosures. No effort was made to learn which types of enclosures are effective. Several women mentioned specific items such as towels and other recurring purchases. Others mentioned furniture and appliances bought after seeing a "special" in an enclosure.

Our discussion of department store enclosures, either to charge customers or others, is not related in any sense to monthly bill enclosures. While unpleasant associations of the monthly bill might seem negative, the expected monthly bill may have more acceptance than other mail reaching the home. Because a considerable percentage of all monthly statements reflect diminishing balances on budget accounts, the statement carrying this news has an advantage in being the first to suggest the "next purchase." That is especially true for furniture and large appliance time purchases.

EFFECTIVENESS OF ENCLOSURES: FEW RESULT IN SALES

In asking housewives their feelings about bill enclosures, they were asked how they usually learned of bargains offered in the department stores. Almost all of them named daily newspapers, although perhaps one in ten responded that stores "send out flyers when they have bargains." A majority said they shopped when they wanted an item.

As with all mail inquiries made to housewives, most of these respondents said that too much mail comes to their homes. But there was no pattern in how they responded to it. Some said that they "read everything," while others said they read nothing except "bills and personal letters." The conclusion reached through this small survey is that department store mailings still have a fairly easy road to finding a reader. Except for bill enclosures, the "free goods" (merchandise coupons, etc.) were the only ones receiving a majority report from these homes. Even though some large-ticket items were reported purchased through offers coming with monthly statements, major evidence is that items of high frequency purchase have by far the best response. A final question asked each housewife was, "Have you ever received a personal or general letter from one of your department stores?" Not one respondent said that she had.

NEW SITUATIONS IN LARGE STORE MERCHANDISING

Our discussion of the personalized letter for department and other large, old-line stores, is based on the supposition that some have attempted such mailings and abandoned them. We know that women will read most any mail they receive. We believe that two new situations in large store merchandising may have come into focus since any great number of stores have tried personalized letters.

These situations are 1) the growth of new self-service bargain type stores and 2) the increase in consumer spending for services as opposed to products.

INCREASING APPEAL OF DEPARTMENT STORE SERVICES

The older low-price store of chain or mail-order companies has increasingly appealed to payment customers. The newer type has its greatest appeal to cash buyers, but for higher-priced items they go after long-term payment buyers. Historically, none of these types of competition to the old-line department store has offered "services" extensively. The time is near when in the chain department store field some estimate that one third of their volume will result from services.

Department stores, in attaining their dominance and customer loyalty, have hewed closely to the line of offering most wanted women's wear and ample displays of almost every type of household need. Most have depended on their realistic merchandising techniques geared to seasonal demand planning to sustain their sales share when combined with the "easiest to reach" downtown shopping center—the department store itself. Also, a majority of department stores have followed the market into shopping centers in the suburbs. Here they frequently dominate as they do in downtown areas, but they must continuously re-evaluate all of their advertising and promotion methods. In these competitive shuffles none can sit still on past proved techniques.

SUBURBAN SHIFTS AND DISCOUNT STORES AFFECT CUSTOMER LOYALTY

A new experience for some transplanted department stores is to be the newcomer in suburban areas where small local merchants have dominated. Experience is showing that customer loyalty is not deep for long established merchants in suburbs. By the same token, changing product lines and offerings of services have dimmed the customer's familiarity with famous department stores. The self-service and discount stores may have a long road to acceptance as sources of higher-priced apparel, but with food and low-priced children's wear they gain broad exposure for all offerings to families normally dependent on the well-established quality store in whatever location. All bets are off as far as "past reputations" controlling buying.

PERSONALIZED LETTERS TO STRENGTHEN QUALITY IMAGE

Someplace in the "revolutionary" mixture of changes in locations and lines, "bargain images" and the rest, some new techniques are in waiting. One such newer technique, personalized letters to upper-income homes, can have a unique value in strengthening consumer awareness of the "institutional" aspect of the department store as the community quality center.

Personalized letters from large stores with well-known names must present a hard, complete proposition. An "institutional" appeal would be "aiding the enemy." But it must be based on what the older store does best—services. Unlike the bill enclosure, this communication is unexpected. It will depend for readership on the value of its proposition just as a newspaper advertisement does. While its essence should be to revitalize the sounder image-value, it should not attempt to merchandise "bargains." Personalized letters do not replace enclosures. If the letters carry any enclosures, they should be confined to one piece. The enclosure is at best incidental here. Planning letters is our job.

PLANNING PERSONALIZED LETTERS TO UPPER INCOME HOMES

Suppose we plan to send a personalized letter from our president to all current and five-year past charge customers. Let us emphasize our "service" in each letter. While the decision as to frequency will rest to some extent on the type of letters sent and the objectives of the program, at its outset we might try mailings every 90 days. That coincides with seasons, and it obviates the doubts regarding the letters being nuisances to homes conscious of the great flow of unnecessary mail.

DEFINING QUALITY POSITION

The first basic objective of our letters is to strengthen the department store's long-standing image as a service source for quality merchandise and values. That will not supplant the need for a specific offering, but it gives the quality store a chance to define its quality position. The older department stores must keep alive an awareness of their prestige. From their viewpoint they sell non-advertised items to store visitors because the shopper "saw the item when in the store." From the customer's viewpoint that purchase is explained this way, "I bought this because I have always wanted a ——— from that store." The store's prestige is frequently strong enough that one of its garment labels is shifted to two or three coats before being discarded. All department store officials know dramatic cases of store name value.

Unfortunately, name value requires more fertilizing than any other quality. Posed against bait advertisements of newer self-service stores, quality offerings seldom win. Even fear of a low-priced label grows dimmer as non-prestige stores plan their offerings around well-known brands. Advertising in newspapers with the "prestige look" must pay its way with offerings that out-pull the bargain store. Department stores cannot buy generally circulated media to re-seed prestige. But the hard core of higher economic customers that retain year-after-year relationships is far from impervious to bargains. This market may aggregate 10 to 15 percent of a community's homes, and the personalized letter is the way to influence it at a compatible cost.

STRATEGY OF "UNEXPECTED" LETTERS

In outlining the situations into which we can fit personalized letters from department stores to homes, our aim is to establish that there is a value in "unexpected" letters to consumers even where they already receive considerable mail from the store.

The strategy of sending the unexpected letter is widely different than enclosing an offering with the statement. The encloures have an established meaning that customers get to know. They characteristically offer items wanted at the time they arrive and in addition to an attractive price they inform that a good supply is available. A personalized letter may leave its reader wondering why it was sent. Its purpose is not to supplant enclosures nor advertised values. The objective of the personalized letter should adhere closely to one of the situations outlined above or some other condition involving the customer. Letters must always answer the question, "What does it do for me?"

ACHIEVING STORE PRESTIGE

The most serious need that can be met by personalized letters is that related to store prestige. We need merely state that under normal circumstances a considerable accumulated value in all store advertising is its impact for later purchases. While the term prestige may not fully describe this retained image that brings customers into stores six months after they have seen an advertisement, no other type of store has that long-retained power in anything near the same degree. Prestige is the core of "store image." The large store that can creditably say, "world famous," has in that term a great value. To its customers that term is much more impelling than "money back."

A final condition should be introduced before we get to the business of framing our personalized letter into specific objectives. This condition is that our store does display and sell merchandise and services that have established prestige value. These would include imports in "collection" groupings, travel items geared to luxury, educational products or items whose volume potentials are so low that a family would not expect to find them. Example: red-checked tablecloths.

VALUES IN STOCKING LUXURY LINES

It would be less than realistic if we did not start our discussion by agreement that in the trade the appeal of a great many stores' prestige name is strictly pie-in-the-sky. Shoppers look but buy elsewhere. On the other hand, stores that carry quality lines not available to bargain stores have a tangible value that can be, for the store, an advantage when offered in direct competition to items priced on large volume. Were it possible for a majority of medium-to-upper income families to see national prestige magazines monthly, department stores carrying lines shown would have their re-fertilization need. With that clue, we can start to outline our objectives.

MATERIALS AND SIZE OF PERSONALIZED LETTERS

Materials for our personalized letter should include embossed executive stationery. In appearance it should resemble letters that are sent by the store president to other executives.

Mechanically, our letter should be processed so that none but an expert could observe that it was not personally written to one customer. Its length should be one or two pages. The two-page letter is preferable, but we must let our proposition determine its length. From the viewpoint of readers' time available, our letter could be ten pages; the limitation is that we would lose impact were we to include the many elements that length indicates. If the letter is good looking, the length is immaterial. To make it too short would be wasteful because we cannot "load" it with enclosures. The exceptions to the rule of no enclosures with personalized letters limit such matter to one piece.

MAKE A CONCRETE OFFER

The first caution we should observe in "prestige letters" is that they must have a visible working load. Prestige is our motive. It is not our product or service. Our letter need not offer a specific product, but it must offer something concrete. Our objective is not to have our name better known, nor tell our location. The opening must tell our full proposition. We do not want to insert any questions, nor do we want to get added attention by exclamations or shock terms.

PREPARATION AND COMPOSITION OF SELLING LETTERS

The rule for preparation and composition of selling letters is that we first define our objectives as they relate to the customer's interest. This may be arrived at through a process of elimination. For example, in analyzing potential business losses that might be averted were our customers more conscious of the differences between the department store and the discount image store, we must not indicate that we are aware of that store as competition. This rules out any implication that we are "best in the long run."

Dear Mrs. Jones:

In selecting the resort wear for offerings to our customers this season, we have departed from a past practice to meet the needs of those leaving late in the season as well as for those departing early. We have arranged with several of our fashion and sportswear houses to ship portions of our orders from week to week throughout the entire season. In this manner, you will have full selections here throughout the season, even though your departure is delayed into March.

While the foregoing may not parallel verbiage common to letters of its type, the "prestige store" viewpoint is clearly illustrated. It does several things:

1. While it would go to a wide segment of the customers, it assumes that they will "winter vacation." The growth of winter vacations is a growing business potential for at-home stores.
2. No store of quality can assume that a fast-growing bargain will not carry winter resort fashion and sportswear.
3. Resorts frequently aim advertising at non-markets to establish prestige image among neighbors of their customers. A personal letter from a store that assumes a winter vacation can be gratifying to stay-at-homes.
4. Volume stores in the discount field could not write such a proposition.
5. Resort operators know that there is a specific "late season market," developing as the regulars leave. This market is bargain-conscious and bears kinship to the the after-season market. Information that "good selections" are available in late season has meaning as shopping interest and as an economy potential.

The example we are using does not lend itself to a highly cohesive, compact statement. However, our aim should be to put our entire proposition into the minimum number of sentences. The opening of this letter should be confined to the proposition. If we are speaking to this customer in a vein suggesting that she is thought to be a winter vacationer, she will not lose interest merely because her family vacation is two weeks in mid-summer.

Winter vacations and their accoutrements are as close to a universal luxury symbol as America has. Before mid-20th Century they were not sufficiently established to have that acceptance. Those who leave home in mid-winter for a resort trip retain a proprietary interest in such commodities throughout the year. Those who stay home have reasons other than no interest for their non-purchase. Whether a proposition similar to our example is suited to a specific store, it embodies the elements and technique that spell prestige.

YOUR LETTER BODY VALIDATES YOUR OFFER

To continue our example into the body of the letter, we should pause to review exactly what the body of a selling letter should do. The burden of the letter's body is to tell how and why the offer is valid or meaningful. Even though our basic proposition fits the customer's need to a "T," it must be far more justified before it will change a thinking pattern or attitude. Should we have our letter reach a store customer who is planning on going to Florida in March, we have the ideal recipient. But she may have thought before the letter arrived that vacation or resort wear always arrived in stores throughout the season. In hanging our proposition on a later purchase, we lose an opportunity to spur action.

We must bear in mind that few appeals accomplish more than one objective. Our aim here is to set our store apart from a competitive type of store. With that in mind, let us compose a letter body to follow the opening in our example.

"It was not many years ago when our volumes of these types of wear were not sufficient to justify more than one showing each season. With the great increase each year in winter travel, we find that many of our customers prefer travel in the late season. Also, we have learned that types of garments not always wanted at the start of the season become in great demand later.

"Perhaps most important to all of us is that early in the season peak shipments put a considerable load on all of our suppliers. By having our requirements spread over the season, we are able to schedule shipments after the peak season. In this manner some of the values in the later-arriving selections are outstanding. In any event, we can assure you that whenever you should plan departure for a winter trip, we will have full selections of things you will want."

In those paragraphs we have justified our letter. We have given a reason not formerly present for writing now. We have assumed that she might have a problem finding new things late in the season. Above all, we have put ourselves into a position parallel to hers. We have suggested savings late in the season.

THE CLOSE TELLS RECEIVER WHAT TO DO NEXT

To wind up this letter we should tell her what to do next. That is always the purpose of the close of a letter. We can assume that interest in her trip is excited by our letter. What does she do about it? Or in most cases where this letter arrives in the home, there is no winter trip coming. What do those women do?

The basic purpose of our letter is to tell our customers that we have services not available at lesser stores. But we haven't made a good case unless we can give our message real meaning for the majority who will receive it.

Almost equal in importance to its message is the signature of the head of the company at the bottom of the letter. Regardless of other considerations, the president or local store manager should sign personalized letters. If he is active at the store, he is invariably active in the community, either civically or socially. Should someone other than the store corporate head, or local manager be "best known," that will be an exception.

PERSONALIZED LETTER WRITING PROCEDURES

As with other advertising, the general manager or president will not compose the letter. But similarly to commercial letters, he will read it after it is prepared, and re-dictate it. This technique is explained at length in another chapter. The source of material for a store personalized letter should be similar to that for store-wide advertising. Once the basic materials are determined, they should be put into "copy." In turn, this original copy would be approved by the merchandising manager or whoever ordinarily approves store copy. After the merchandising and advertising departments are satisfied with the letter, it should go to the head of the company for re-dictating. The amount of editing required after the company head has rewritten it would be determined by the quality of the letter.

The importance of having the president re-cast any personalized letter is simply that he is responsible for the major direction of the store's growth. If he is fairly active, he becomes familiar to some degree with many of the influential people of the community. There are important names on the list to which the letter goes. If it were going to a single important family in town, he would expect to dictate it. The value of reflecting his viewpoint, manner and personality cannot be discounted if we wish to draw families closer to the store.

PROMOTING THE STORE'S UNIQUE ATTRIBUTES

In discussing the value of personalized letters to families that know the department store well, our aim is to suggest the promotion of the unique attributes of the store. The most dramatic of these is the store's inventory of quality merchandise and quality services. To the customer that is the basis of a proud relationship. She enjoys telling strangers that her department store supplies outstanding things. It strengthens her habit of judging national brands by which local store carries them. The personalized letter telling her specific services and seasonal products adds to her conviction that the store is unique.

In the foregoing we have not attempted to do more than indicate methods of determining objectives. The letters themselves must follow the technique of good letters. Many department stores have writers who can convert attractive general messages into letters. Elsewhere in these notes considerable discussion of letter elements is devoted to all types of letters. Rather than add to that here, we might close this discussion by examining the relationship between the value of the old-fashioned store and that of the fresh new youthful appeal store that pays slight heed to the past.

In store merchandising groupings, the shop within a store has proved the value of the age or use-function relationships. It is not altogether an accident that most of these "shops" are devoted to items appealing to the younger markets. Younger persons spend more time on the streets, where many young marrieds are employed and in shopping centers. They are more curious, and they devote more time to planning and thinking about purchases. Without attempting to enter into discussing general semantics, the term "old fashioned" is terrifically negative with young people. They shun it as they do "middle age."

LETTERS TO YOUNG MARRIEDS

The paradox of younger women seeking "fashion without money" is based on their relatively limited willingess to spend. Most have a family with plans. This has led to a "smart to buy discount" momentum that gives an undue advantage to "bargain" stores which only infrequently stock merchandise suited to style and fashion-minded women. This market might well respond to personalized letters aimed at "open-end . . . accounts." The fresh and original approach is definitely and closely allied to consciousness of quality. The burden of letters to young marrieds, most of whom are both employed, is to establish that the store's objective is close to their problem. A letter does not mention "your problems." That is not only negative, it is a dangerous assumption. Their problems are perhaps overwhelming, but don't try to guess what they are.

The broad ever-present objective of all personalized letters from stores should be to tighten the bond. Our aim is to retain the value of being the place where most of their needs can be met; our problem is to be aware of keeping a newness factor in whatever we offer. Direct-to-home salesmen have long demonstrated that when you develop a sale at home you have little or no competition. Our letters from the head of the company are read as a unique appeal. Their message is not compared to another offering. While that omits shopping, it tells the customer of a service without doing so in unison with competitors. And if our letter is effective, it adds greatly to any other possible appeal to make the family feel their bond to the store.

CHAPTER XIV

DEALERS' CUSTOMER RELATIONS

The Sales Letter on Service

Consumer durable products carry warranties that generally are uniform in their industries. One manufacturer may introduce an extended warranty one season and the next season the others either follow or he may discontinue it. In the search for competitive advantage, automobiles, appliances, television-radio and others who have long-expectancy products have grown in warranty complexities. Some products carry warranties on a part-by-part schedule. Most warranties have in common that the customer pays for the "labor." Sometimes householders feel that the service man invents "needs" for parts not covered by the warranty.

In experience with many commodities, the "bargain-burnt" purchaser thereafter "knows her dealer." With appliances the best known stores frequently are easier to blame than newer discount stores. The "discounter" seldom sells a private label major appliance. His product service is very often more than some customers expected when they made the purchase. Among the aspects of "service cynicism" is a feeling that one's best bet is to buy the best product and hope for the best.

Automobile dealers selling lower-priced cars fulfill the checkups covered by the warranty, then see no more of a majority of their buyers until they are ready to trade again. That is not necessarily negative. Some dealers prefer "complainers" find a repair shop elsewhere. They have an exclusive franchise, sell no other major product and their shops are set up to "pay the overhead" on the entire physical plant with no more than a fraction of their purchasers returning for service. This pattern has been established for at least a business generation. The large manufacturers support their dealers' service with national advertising, but except for upper-price range cars, no dealers' service shortcomings are greatly damaging to new car sales.

Appliance service and sales have always been greatly more tied to each other. Because manufacturers have developed service organizations even the rankest price-cutters supply that coverage to a degree not differing from "quality image" stores. Similar to the car service, appliance service is available for those who are willing to pay. The cost is basically the reason appliance purchasers condemn service. Generally speaking, most discount stores feel as car dealers do regarding service. They supply the factory-sponsored coverage and it is available as long as the customer uses the appliance. The prices may increase as the warranty is outlived, but no one is without a service agency to call. Their customers are prone to looking for a service man whose prices are lower. They frequently feel that the savings were made with the purchase. Department stores and to a considerable extent all non-bargain image stores whose sustenance lines are not appliances, have a different relationship with customers. Likewise, appliance dealers who live off sales and service occupy still another attitude relationship.

COMMERCIAL LETTERS FORTIFY DEALER REPUTATIONS

The need for commercial letters to fortify the store's reputation is confined to the middle group mentioned above—quality-type stores which sell appliances to regular customers for other merchandise. A discount store may be highly ethical and conscientious but to volunteer any service that would add a cost would defeat his profit method. He knows that purchasers are coming to him seeking price first. Past irritations did not deter them. At the other extreme, the independent appliance dealer lives off his sales-service relationship. He stays close to service call incidence, and to his costs and prices. He likes to "play ball" with customers and he is always working to sell them their next appliance. That leaves the department, furniture, hardware, music and other quality-minded stores as the victims of the "service cynicism." They need a technique to keep in touch with appliance buyers. Even where these stores meet prices of discount stores on appliances, their long-time customers expect attention. They do not switch to "bargain stores" for other goods, but when they switch to an "independent" service store, they buy their next appliance where they feel a "bargain" is most likely.

LETTERS FOR QUALITY STORE FOLLOW-UP ON SALES

In urging a letter program as a quality-store follow-up for appliance sales, we should recognize that our reason is not essentially to attract the next purchase. Purchasers of refrigerators, freezers, ranges, water heaters and other low-service incidence appliances are practically unaware of service needs. But they are the same families that buy automatic washers, dryers, television-radio and other equipment requiring occasional attention.

PRESIDENT-STATUS LETTERS TO CUSTOMERS

A letter from the president of a big store coming soon after the installation of a refrigerator may seem unwarranted. As an avowal of interest in the purchase, it can be highly effective. Its purpose might be to dramatize the value of dealing with the well-established store. If the purchase is an automatic cycle-type appliance, or TV set, it can reassure a purchaser who may have misgivings.

TIMING FOLLOW-UP LETTERS

In proposing follow-up letters on sales involving service, these are considered "part of the sale," even though the writing program may be planned to include four letters. The first would be sent following installation; another in six months; the third at the end of a year when payments may be completed, and the final letter a year later. This series is the follow-up to protect and build the store's reputation. Should a letter be sent marking the final payment, that would come from the sales department. It might be followed-up by a phone call suggesting another appliance purchase.

PRESIDENT LETTERS TO THE SERVICE GROUP

In addition to the president-status letters to purchasers, similar letters should be directed at the service organization members from the president. These are appeals and reminders that the store's reputation goes with them whenever they answer a service call. As composed letters, all of these should be set up by the appliance department.

HOW TO CONSTRUCT SALES FOLLOW-UP LETTERS

The sales follow-up letter is not simply an amenity even though it is going to a purchaser of a refrigerator. Its make-up must follow the design of your best selling letters. This means that it has a working proposition that makes up the first paragraph. The how and why of your service proposition is explained in the second paragraph and the final or closing paragraph should point back to your store. Let us illustrate:

> Dear Mrs. Johnson:
>
> We all are pleased that you came to our store for your most recent appliance purchase. In making this decision you assured yourself of a sound value, and long-term attention for whatever service needs you may have. We stand behind the manufacturer's warranty with our reputation to see that you get the finest service from this appliance.
>
> Over a great many years our store has stood for quality and service. Our entire organization is formed to take care of your needs whether a purchase is recent or one made some time back. We feel that in your present purchase you have made a wise choice, but in any event we are ready to stand behind it.
>
> May I suggest that whenever you need quality merchandise, either in equipment for your kitchen or laundry, or in children's items, or fashions for yourself, you again give us an opportunity to show what we are offering. This season our stocks are especially full of fine merchandise. It would be our pleasure to serve you again very soon.
>
>   Sincerely,

The housewife rounding out 15-months use of an automatic washer with nine months of payments ahead is easy to placate when the machine fails. They all fail on Monday, it seems, and the service man never gets there till Thursday. When he has repaired the machine his bill may be $5 for labor, with no charge for the part. But the housewife is mad. How would a letter help?

SERVICE PROPOSITIONS BEFORE THE SALE

Let us examine letters related to service before the sale. In keeping with our other recommendations, this type of communication involves a series of letters planned as to method and objective before the first one is sent. Let us start with a well-known appliance dealer. He decides to send a letter to one thousand major appliance or TV-radio or phono buyers gleaned from the previous year. These letters should be personalized. Sent locally, after being processed by a letter house, they may cost him 20 cents each. Example:

Dear Mrs. Jones:

"A year ago you made an important purchase at our store. It was important to us, even though you may have made others later. I looked up your purchase because I am interested in knowing how well it is serving you.

"Our policy is to go beyond carrying out the manufacturers' warranty. Almost always we are able to do it, even when it may cause us to lose an original sale. We are among the few these days who supply our own service. We would prefer to do this right rather than sell you 'cut prices' then dollar you for upkeep. The only limitation is when a product comes along that seems to 'break down.' When we find one of these among our customers, we try to replace it on the terms best suited to the customer's need.

"I do not want to create the impression that we want to 'give away' our service or products. We have been here some time, and we plan to stay. But I make no bones about it, I think you're entitled to lots of attention when something goes wrong and you should not have to wait more than a day when it does. Please let me know how well you have been taken care of. We want your next purchase and we want to earn it now."

"UNEXPECTED" LETTERS TO AIM AT THE NEXT PURCHASE

Stores investing $400 in that letter should expect great benefits. When the store is in a city of more than 50,000 population its customers may have bought most of their other appliances from competitors. A householder who owns seven units—kitchen, laundry and television—very likely has had service altercations with one or more dealers. The chances are that none of these has written her on this subject. So she is favorably impressed that you did. You are vague regarding the date and type of appliance she purchased, but she is not aware of that.

After the "unexpected" letter shows your interest in service, be careful not to overdo it. Your letter puts you on record and if her husband sees it he very likely will say, "it pays to buy from a good dealer."

Discount and other high-volume stores seldom attempt to deal personally with customers. Surveys show that women identify themselves as "department store" customers but rarely as discount store customers. Older-established merchants should bear in mind that customers expect more of them than they do of discount stores. Discount stores take the business on price. But the more prone to product-service an item is, the less likely the discount store is to carry it. But their image is so close to "bargain" that post-sale demands are not as great as on department stores.

LETTERS TO FOLLOW-UP SERVICE CALLS

The letter to Mrs. Jones is aimed at "her next purchase." Before suggesting our second letter to her, we should suggest another letter to users who have had service calls this month. Dealers who do not personally go out on service calls are not aware exactly of what happened when the field man went out. The independent dealer must assume that the customer is moderately satisfied unless he learns differently. So he should have a letter to follow up service calls. This letter could well be written in two versions. One should be for customers who bought the appliance from his store; the other for those buying elsewhere and calling him for service. For his own sales he should write:

Dear Mrs. Jackson:

As much as we regret the failure that caused a service call to your home recently, I am writing to thank you for calling us and to express the hope that our services met your expectations.

Our policy is to do more than the manufacturer's warranty. This is not always possible, but we do it that way more often than not.

We have full lines of almost all well-known appliances and television sets on display now. In fact, we are offering specials in all of these because they are in good supply. Just as in the past, we will not try to sell you if you come in. But if you should see an appliance or other item and buy it, we will not forget to keep it in repair after you have it.

I hope you can come in soon.

Yours very truly,

That letter will impress a housewife even though she was not fully satisfied when the service man left. Her husband may see it and remark, "He should give us service at those prices." Even that reaction is not negative.

CONSUMER MOTIVATION IN DEALER, DEPARTMENT STORE AND DISCOUNT STORE SHOPPING

Dealers are realistic on consumer motivation. Distributors are somewhat less so and manufacturers only rarely realistic regarding what causes customers to buy one item, rather than another. Even though they are unhappy later, most families, disappointed after a major purchase from a discount store with the service offered, will go back again if the price is lower. This is being repeated every day in areas near or in large cities. It can only mean that consumers have very little confidence in any dealer's responsibility. Not all customers of discount houses are brushed off. A service call generally brings factory-sponsored or the distributor's product service. That man has no knowledge of the history of the purchase except that it came from a specific store. Most commonly the parts are covered in the warranty. He collects for his labor. She may resist paying but of course she pays. Thereafter, she frequently calls local "service stores."

The irony is that when they want another appliance, they go

back to that store. The service-quandary, as it appears to owners of six or eight major appliances, television, room coolers and floor products is a penalty of ownership.

In all parts of the country there is a basic and widespread pessimism among householders regarding services. Here and there is an island, generally an entire community, where service has been treated as a genuine responsibility, but few of these are near the large cities.

Big stores, well-established with customers from one generation to the next, are invariably the exception. They tell customers that they get service, and it is there. But as new self-service stores increase in numbers, more and more purchasers go to them on the theory of "discount." In many items shoppers find prices higher, but the "image" attracting bargain-seekers is strong.

The answer for department stores is personalized letters. Service itself is highly personal. The family with a broken washer feels that it is the only such unfortunate.

WHEN TO LAUNCH LETTER PROGRAMS

A service letter program should start immediately after the installation. Many small dealers practice this. Such a letter would have as its proposition, "You made a purchase from us, and while we hope you never need us, we are ready to take care of that piece of home equipment whenever you need us. That is our way of operating."

That is a composed letter for the president's signature. It is followed in one year by another. Let us make this one a "birthday" letter.

> Dear Mrs. Jones:
>
> This is the anniversary of the appliance purchase you favored us with a year ago. I hope that it has performed beyond your expectations, with minimum service needs.
>
> At the time I wrote and told you that we try to conduct our appliance business a little differently than some we hear about. I do not have the records before me, but if you needed service at any time, we know that it was there.
>
> As your appliance gets older, some aspects of manufacturer's warranty expire. Then we will need to make a charge if such a part is

needed. I want you know that we will ask you pay only what the manufacturer gets for the part, and as we agree, you will pay for labor. The value of that arrangement is this: the work will be done right, or there will be no charge to correct it. I hope that you do not need us, but if you do we want you to feel good about the way we respond.

The new home equipment: including appliances, television, housewares and air conditioners are now in good supply. We would like to have you come in when it is convenient. Or, if you have a question, call Mr. Johnson, our manager in that department. He will be pleased to serve you.

Please let us know if you have any service needs not promptly handled.

      Sincerely,

Even though there have been irritations over service needs, a letter such as that will restore good will. That customer will cite that letter whenever she hears a friend tell of a service abuse.

CHAPTER XV

THE PERSONAL LETTER
—IN BUSINESS

The Case for the Thank You Note for a Job-Seeking Appointment

Many successful executives will say that the only time they gag up on letter writing is when they attempt a personal one. They feel that a "thank you" note is corny, or unnecessary. They figure a career resumé is more effective than a letter to change jobs and they believe nothing comes of complaint letters. On all counts they are wrong.

Whatever other neglect of customers large corporations may practice, the "thank you" planning is invariably systematized. For the first moves in job changing, the resumé is negative and a good letter almost always necessary. And a good letter is the way to register a product or service complaint.

TIMING THANK YOU LETTERS

We may have a great many occasions requiring letters for personal business, but these three are the most important when we have occasions to use them. The "thank you" letter can make a great deal of difference in our careers. Unlike the other two that we shall consider, their composition is not important. But their timing is very important. There are many overlooked occasions when they might help the sender more than the receiver. These include the informal praise note to an associate, the "thank you" to your superior for some small recognition, and the note to the lower-echelon commending an action or to a customer for an interview. These are amenity letters that may mean little or they may erase a lingering irritation. In personal dealings in home communities, each of us has a great many relationships that involve letter communication. A "thank you" note to a school teacher, a civic volunteer, police or crossing guards or to a fellow committee member does not replace a friendly handshake, but it is always welcome and it can greatly ease our paths in community life.

OBJECTIVITY IS THE THANK YOU LETTER'S STRENGTH

The great strength of a "thank you" letter can lie in its objectivity. The principal composition rule that separates the effective from the others is simply that the receiver becomes the subject. Example: "Your assistance in getting the Drive over the top is greatly appreciated. . . ." Or, "You have my heartfelt thanks for the manner in which. . . ." The "thank you" should be reversed to put the receiver in the "doing position."

PERSONAL NOTES—WHEN IN DOUBT, SEND ONE

For personal "thank you" notes, the subject should be confined to expressing appreciation for the specific service involved. Many well-motivated "thank yous" are nullified by the introduction of too much commercialism. That suggestion applies largely to personal, rather than company letters. We can summarize the case for personal "thank you" notes by saying, "When in doubt, send one." No one is offended by a "thank you." The more you send, regardless of their occasions, the more dividends in good will you will earn as you go. Their cost is small, and their benefits many.

LETTERS RELATED TO JOB CHANGING

At the other extreme in point of incidence is the letter related to changing jobs. Most salary employees change jobs more than once before they settle down and a growing minority is continuing to change after they reach planned objectives. Years ago the "job application" was largely for recent high school graduates. If they landed the job, the aim was to stay for life. Nowadays "business lifers" are becoming extinct. The executive who was once "locked in at 40" now may be awaiting that age to make his next move. The changing attitudes on job-permanence in management are not entirely the employees' doing. In the rise of countless new companies, new merged organizations, and new skill requirements, many corporations could not "bring along" their own candidates fast enough. They went into the market for management and in turn they became the market for the other company—frequently a growing competitor.

PROFESSIONAL MANAGEMENT OPPORTUNITIES AND THE RISE OF "HEAD HUNTERS"

This enterprise for "experience" initiated by employers has been welcomed by a rising class of candidates sometimes described as "professional management" who are available for levels from electronic data processing analysts to company presidents. They may have listened to the long-term outlooks of campus recruiters, but their eyes were on their second or third moves. In turn a new service industry has grown up to serve companies requiring experience for which the old-line management training program did not provide and to serve the rising executive whose skills may be better utilized in a new location. These management consultants and executives search organizations, work from opposite sides of the street, and serve a very real need. With the high incidence of job-changing, its growing acceptance and the improved facilities for "opportunity seekers," the bread and butter aspect of "how to make the move" is as vexing and worrisome as ever. That thousands of career-minded will move is known. How each does it is as much a problem as when it was a rarity.

That gives us the broadest base for recognizing job-changing. In spite of its growth, job-changing is still the exception for executives after their thirtieth birthday. Even as corporations intensify their executive hunt, they fortify the "lock in" benefits: hiring executives is expensive and risky. But foregoing pension benefits is secondary to ambitious executives when an "executive search" agency approaches them. Widely publicized as this technique of procuring "experience" is, it does not scratch the surface of the vast army "hoping" for a job change, but it is almost unfailing in bringing forth a resumé from executives from field specialists to corporate presidents.

NEVER SEND A RÉSUMÉ FIRST

The rise of the résumé accompanied the growth of the salary-job change rate. For personnel files, executive placement files and for purposes of screening a group of qualified candidates, this specification sheet is invaluable. For even remotely encouraging interest except where a specific job is to be filled, they are damaging. When you are seeking to change positions, you will rarely improve yourself by matching your statistics against the field.

LETTERS: NUMBER ONE METHOD TO INITIATE A JOB CHANGE

The number one method of starting a position-changing effort is a letter asking for an appointment. Many executives who "file a résumé" with a placement office are fearful of writing directly to a company. Or after they are on notice of employment termination they start a letter, "I am considering changing positions in a desire for something offering more future growth opportunity than my present position. I have discussed this with my superiors to keep my intention aboveboard." That fools no one. They know you have sixty days to find something.

In suggesting that we start today with the simplest form of letter, a "thank you" note to un-gag ourselves, the inference is not that our grammar needs improvement. The organization of our material, the freedom of expression and familiarity with the readers' viewpoint are the reasons we must practice self-related writing. With all we know regarding ourselves, none of us can envisage what will interest the other fellow until we write it.

UNEMPLOYED EXECUTIVE LETTERS

The executive who is out of a position, for whatever reason, should not send qualifying facts to prospective employers. He had much better sign in with a placement office as his first move. Then he should write some letters to secure interviews. These "interview" letters well could be the most important letters he will ever write:

> Dear Mr. Vice President:
>
> If I may take the liberty of introducing myself to you in this manner; I am writing to secure a personal interview with you at your convenience.
>
> In the industry your programs are generally known, and mentioned favorably, wherever people discuss its affairs. For that reason I wish to impose on your time to discuss the possibility of becoming a member of your organization.
>
> I am not writing to your personnel executive because I am a marketing executive in the field organization of a member-company in the industry; not a direct competitor.
>
> Since I joined the industry with my present employer six years ago, in the marketing training department, and later as assistant to the Atlanta Division Manager, it has been in my mind to come some day and talk to you about working for you. My major in graduating from Indiana University was marketing. Coming directly to my present employer, I have gained solid ground during these years when I have married and since had children. Now I feel ready to solicit the opportunity to make the type of change I look to as final for me.
>
> I have had no occasion to mention this request to my associates or others, but you may feel free to enquire regarding my general character. Should you be able to see me and after the interview encourage me to formally apply, you will find my references in first-rate order with my employer, Acme Electric Company.
>
> Thank you for whatever consideration you may be able to give this request.
>
> Sincerely,

TECHNIQUES FOR JOB INTERVIEW LETTERS

The proposition, when an executive writes to a company officer with whom he is not acquainted, is the request for an interview. To state that again: The proposition is *not your qualifications,* in requests for interviews with company officers with whom you are not acquainted. The *proposition is the request.*

As with all "unexpected" letters, the body tells the hows and whys. No one can secure a good position from a stranger by means of a letter. He can secure an interview only. And if the sought-after executive is busy, getting the interview, as a stranger, will be quite a trick.

The close is pointing to how he can proceed. That should clarify the petitioner's position regarding confidence. For the writer to say, "please treat this in confidence," would kill the executive's interest. Our writer has said he wants to discuss joining the company. That is not an application. At the end, he says that should he make an application, his present employer references will be in order.

When an applicant says, "my present employers know of this letter," the reader knows the fellow's been fired.

ADDRESS THE "RIGHT" MAN

At the start of our "right man" discussion, we did not use an example showing a job-seeking letter to a president for two reasons: 1) company presidents only infrequently select employees below officer level; 2) letters to presidents should be signed by corporate officers unless they are from customers or acquaintances.

SOURCES OF EXECUTIVE JOBS

Those seeking business positions have four widely-travelled routes to follow: 1) Placement agencies; 2) Letter to company executive personnel manager, or to a company officer; 3) Business page display-classified advertisements, and 4) Through executive-search or management consultants working for the employer.

EXECUTIVE SEARCH ORGANIZATIONS

The last named type of position source tends to meet the needs for department heads, scientists, and engineers; highly trained specialists, marketing executives (including advertising and publicity); and not infrequently new company chief executive officers. These aides to management agents specialize in high-level positions for companies whose needs, possibly intensified by rapid growth, cannot be met within the company. Any salary employee who attracts attention from one of these specialists should listen carefully; and if available, say so with minimum coyness. These professionals know their requirements, and indications of your reluctance to change would tend to be negative, rather than enhancing your bargaining position. The limitation of this source is that only indirectly are they interested in the person seeking change. Their interest is in the employer-company. You may "file your resumé" with one of these agents. Six months later you may receive an inquiry. After that the agent may hear of a candidate better suited for his opening and the new candidate becomes number one. In other words, even though some of these encourage filing resumés, they must come after you. They are good sources to know, but your active moves to change positions should point elsewhere.

EMPLOYMENT AGENCIES

The three other commonly used methods of initiating a job change for established middle-income and upwards salary employees are all means that you pursue actively. Number one is widely recognized as the classic method of securing employment: these are the modern employment agencies. Our interest would be in those engaged in executive placement. In all larger cities one or more of these agencies participates in placing executives, from presidents to office managers, in corporations of all sizes. Statistics are not available, but it can be estimated that they influence more upper-level employment than does any other agency. In the largest cities these specialize by industries, types of skills, and salary-levels. Some specialists seek jobs whose salary minimums are $50,000 annually. So that direction should be our first move.

BUSINESS PAGE DISPLAY ADVERTISEMENTS

Our third method mentioned, "business page advertisements," has greater incidence for technical, engineering or research than for general administrative or management jobs. They are very worthwhile leads, and when one looks favorable, it should be followed up. Usually these have "blind" addresses. The limitation on these is that several hundred others see the same offering, so in a sense you are entering a contest. It might be said that such advertisers get a look at almost everyone actively seeking a position. Inversely, you may place a similar advertisement and theoretically get a look at everyone seeking an executive such as you. Your limitation will be that even though you receive several inquiries, you will need time and possibly travel to follow up.

DEVELOPING A RÉSUMÉ

At the outset you should develop a résumé. That advice is aimed at established salary executives but it applies equally to college graduates not long out of school. A difference in procedure for these two types of position candidates is that the established employee should hold onto his résumé; the recent graduate may, and perhaps should, send it to everyone in whom he has an interest.

Your résumé should be a reverse chronological listing of terminal dates from your present position back to birth. You should place near the top of the first page, "(Not an application)." Before you give anyone a copy of your résumé, you should have enough information on its destination so that you can accompany it with a letter.

Before we discuss "use of résumé," we should amplify that most larger companies have a specialized officer in charge of salary or executive personnel. When you are considering writing to a company officer you should not only bear this in mind, you should consider writing to that individual. You can most easily learn his identity by placing a telephone call to the personnel department of the company and asking for his name and title. You need not identify yourself to get this information.

WHEN TO WRITE EXECUTIVE PERSONNEL OFFICERS

We might estimate that more than nine of ten executive-level employees joining any larger companies must pass muster by the executive personnel officer before a final decision. He frequently has resources for quick verification of your statements.

AS A RULE, ALWAYS WRITE THE DEPARTMENT HEAD FIRST

In spite of the inevitability of the personnel officer whom you will meet, if yours is a non-technical job requirement (such as field sales, or market research) you are best advised to write to the officer department head. In fact, should events lead you to the executive personnel head and he informs you that no changes are contemplated and that there are no openings, you should go ahead and write to the departmental officer just the same.

To further point up that advice: even though you may hear of an opening with the direction that you apply to the personnel officer, it is still better to make your first inquiry by letter to the vice president who heads the department. The exception would be if your position is classified as "clerical."

SAVE YOUR RÉSUMÉ FOR INTERVIEWS— MAKE IT THE CLOSER

The résumé should be considered as a "closer," in a letter or sales presentation. There are very few statistical listings of events in your life that are as imposing as your personality or as convincing as a good letter. As pointed out earlier, the request for an interview is your letter proposition; in that same vein, the résumé is your "closer," after you have had the interview. Where an agency is acting for you, the résumé must be filed with him. But do not file the résumé without writing at the top: "Not an Application."

> Dear Department Head:
>
> The undersigned has decided to make a change from his present position as a field representative of a national major appliance manufacturer to a similar organization which is considering filling a field position as a district manager or as an assistant manager in a territory in the Northeastern states. The reason for seeking change is that acceptance of such advancement with my present employer would require leaving the area, which is not possible for personal family reasons.
>
> My employment started in 1953 when I graduated from Purdue University. I started with my present employer in the Market train-

ing department. My first assignment was as a staff member for a product manager, a year later.

In 1956 I was assigned to the New York Northeastern Division Sales office as office assistant, and in 1957 I was promoted to field representative, calling on distributors and others in New Jersey.

During the five years in my present assignment my district has had a sales increase of 24 percent. The overall company increase is approximately 5 percent. Upon three occasions the question of advancement has been opened with me. In each instance a move would have involved leaving the area where I now reside. My wife's mother's dependency on her daughter in extreme old age is the basis for my present adherence to this area. We consider this dependence temporary within the next five years.

In offering divisional manager assignments to me, my superiors have commended my record for administration of my territory. Personally, I consider my greatest strength to be my ability to get along well with the most irascible associates. For example, one of our long-term distributors in a larger city had refused to cooperate on seasonal tie-in promotions for many years prior to my second year in the territory. He grudgingly conceded to "try me out" that year and has since become enthusiastic for these activities. My technique was simply appealing to his sportsmanship: a dare.

My pride in getting along with people traces to my college activities. I was moderately active on campus, although time was limited by employment to earn my board and room.

In addition to my wife, my family includes two children, ages three and six months. It would be a privilege to have an interview directed toward making an application.

      Sincerely,

      John Jones
      Field Representative
      General Appliance Corporation
      560 Lexington Avenue
      New York, N.Y.

CHAPTER XVI

HOW TO DECIDE
WHICH OFFICER TO ADDRESS

Industrial, technical and business selling by commercial letters has some advantages in reaching known markets over consumer correspondence. These advantages are concentrated in the product's inherent relationship to its market. However, once a product is known in these market places, the problems related to expanding sales to non-users are complex. In consumer sales the market may be obscure, but the approach is clear. It's a question of addressing either a man or his wife.

PRESIDENT-TO-PRESIDENT LETTERS: WHEN TO SEND THEM

For commercial letters to establish corporate or product identity, announce programs, or reveal corporate objectives, the president-status letter can be one of the most effective tools known to marketing, because we know it was sent to the "right" man. President-to-president letters generally are self-suggesting when we have determined our proposition. One president's letterhead is treated with respect in the other's office as long as he does not take advantage of the privilege. Taking advantage could be enclosing sales literature or writing to the chief executive as if he were a buyer. That is a mis-use of privilege and it does not work.

Throughout our letter discussions we frequently suggest addressing the president when we are sending commercial letters. While that is advice that we shall not back away from, it does not mean sending him any kind of a message that would be desirable for the purchasing agent, chief engineer or financial officer. And instances where you can enclose printed matter to chief officers are extremely rare.

LETTERS TO UNFAMILIAR COMPANIES

In some of our examples it may seem that we are advocating, "when in doubt, address the president." In one sense this is true. That is, if your company has a worthwhile proposition that hinges on cost-reduction or profit enhancement and you want to get into a company not now on your list, your president should address a letter to the head of any company you are ready to go after. This is not changed by the size of the prospect company.

Another facet of the "unfamiliar company" is one that seems logical as a customer, but one you have not been selling. Every producer in given industries has some non-buyers or non-users among companies that sound logical, but where no order has been forthcoming. Many of these appear on representatives' reports as prospects, but they don't order. These certainly are in line for a president-to-president letter.

REACHING THE RIGHT EXECUTIVE

Unrelated to any inherent reason, we sometimes suggest a means of attracting and holding a president's attention simply because it is usually difficult to do. A letter to a chief engineer on a subject proper to his function and status need only set forth its proposition with an unmistakeable and reasonable request or suggestion as to what we want. Letters, when they are addressed to the right executive, never have difficulty getting readership at the departmental level. But there is a great big area of darkness as to which is the right executive once we go below the president's office. Typical large companies have more than one hundred executive responsibility classifications. A letter to a district manager, general accounting, must not be aimed at the same target as one to district manager, sales training.

COMMERCIAL LETTERS BETWEEN LARGE COMPANIES

Among larger industrial companies marketing executives do not long remain in the dark as to whom they call on. This is what the purchasing agent is for. The sales seeker need only call him or he can go unannounced, if his product or services fits their requirements. In discussing commercial letters between these larger companies of comparable size, there is a considerable area where commercial letters could do a great deal more than is being done by sales executives. Sales seekers learn early in the game that calling on the purchasing agent gets them courteous treatment, but little else. Most of these companies have more than one channel through which orders may be placed or sales information dispensed. The question of reaching the right executive is admittedly the crux.

PRESIDENT-STATUS LETTERS FIT MOST SITUATIONS

We can assume that most of our readers analyzing the "right man" question are agreed that a president-to-president letter can be evolved to fit almost any situation. It may be ironic, but with all the disadvantages smaller companies live with in approaching larger ones, when it comes to a letter from the president of a smaller company to a larger one, the smaller company has some advantages. One of these is that he can assume that the recipient is not familiar with his product, indeed, not even with his company. The larger company to equally large company requires careful amenity-treatment of generally known facts commonly known regarding each.

 Inquiry among 35 company presidents' secretaries disclosed the unfortunate fact that smaller companies writing to chief executives or larger companies make some horrible errors of judgment. Among these is enclosing a postage-paid return envelope. Never enclose anything in a commercial president-status letter.

ASSEMBLING SPECIALIZED EXECUTIVE MAILING LISTS

The most direct manner for commercial letter planners to start assembling a mailing list of specialized executives whose interests may coincide with their offerings is to approach the editor or publisher of a technical or business magazine. The publishing industry supports upwards of 4,000 specialized publications covering everything from accountants to yachtsmen. These publications go to every type of enterprise known, from motoring AAA to civic YWCA.

PROBLEMS IN LOCATING "FUNCTIONAL" EXECUTIVES

If yours is an electronic product, you still may not have a clear view of your "functional executive" after you have learned where he might be located. For example, electronic data processing has placed specialists in that field in almost every type of company in the nation. Engineering can have not less than a dozen functionally unrelated classifications in a single division of a large company. Business magazine publishers sometimes contend that no one can reach any considerable segment of some functional specialists in any manner except the business magazine's pages. Certainly that is the lowest-priced method of reaching the largest number. At the other extreme, the highest-priced method is making direct calls. Of course, they are entirely different levels, or types of marketing. In all but extremely small companies, both should be used. Then letters should be rifle-shot into every prospective office. The only way a letter can damage you is if it is a poor letter, or sent to the wrong executive.

MIS-DIRECTED LETTERS

It can be estimated that mis-directed letters, those not addressed to the most logical executive, are most negative if they hang their hat on "operational aspects." That is to say, never suggest to an advertising director that he select the pencils or typewriter ribbons. In some degree that applies to every status executive throughout most organizations. Industrial relations administrators know the horrors of omitting "climate" from positions. These specialists in bruised feelings know how much more important is status than pay check.

PLANNING COMMERCIAL LETTERS—USING SERVICE AGENCIES

In planning commercial letters the problems tend to concentrate in those aspects that must be surmounted before the message can be composed. Although obstacles invariably include some element of addressee identification or name-availability, there are established service agencies to turn to. In addition to the technical or trade publications, every larger city has letter houses which have access to highly specialized mailing lists. Some lists may designate all of the Rhode Island Red hatchers. Or inquiry might make available names of readers of the Oregon Egg Producers' magazine, the *Eggsaminer;* or even the 5,000 readers of *Gobbles,* the magazine of the Minnesota Turkey Growers Association.

DIRECT MAIL ADVERTISING AGENCIES

In addition to letter houses, many larger cities have specialized direct mail advertising agencies that assist in mailing preparations and mailing lists. These service organizations will start with your description of the market you seek. It may be field support engineers in defense systems departments. The executive you should reach here may be a senior engineer in the defense department or a technical engineer in the missile-space department. No effort is being made deliberately to confuse these prospects for a commercial letter. These three suggested recipients are selected at random from a list of approximately 50 governmental work industrial classifications in a large company.

LEARNING NAMES AND TITLES

A very practical first step to learn names and titles of specific functional assignments in large organizations is to learn the name of the organization manager. This office is responsible for studies related to job descriptions in a majority of the larger companies. Your letter to this office, listing the functions desired, will invariably be answered in a manner that will guide you practically. In some instances company policy dictates that supplier-type letters be addressed simply, "Purchasing Agent," or a similar designation. For our purpose this may be effective in the long run, but our intention here is to determine whom we should address and how we identify him by title.

Where sales calls are made on any size company there is no problem of either getting names or learning which executive might have an interest. Difficult though it is to get name information from many field representatives, they invariably can secure it if they wish to. Manufacturers' reps and distributors frequently do not wish to disclose their "contacts" to any of their product sources. Nonetheless, securing names that are effective within companies generally is easier through direct in-person requests than any other means, if you have a representative who wants to cooperate.

It should be pointed out that assembling names is a costly process and however you secure a mailing list it will cost something. Some list-owners make names available only on a basis of their performing the mailings for you. Or they may release the list to you at double the fee for mailing for you. Obviously these sources have experience in "losing" lists to renters.

SENDERS ALWAYS ADDRESS COUNTERPARTS: V.P. TO V.P.

In starting our examination of how to decide which officer to address, we said the president is a good bet, if our president is signing the letter. By the same token, the vice president of purchasing (or procurement or materials) is a sure bet for our vice president of marketing. Sometimes office-kidders poke fun at advertising agencies or insurance brokers who seem to name everyone a vice-president. The general tone of this analysis of "right man" to address gives some hint as to how handy a vice president title can be.

We might further amplify the obvious by suggesting that a transportation equipment seller can always address the head of the traffic department and media representatives can easily address the top man related to advertising. The weakness of these suggestions is related to their application to the type of commercial letter we are discussing. That type is letters to companies upon whom we do not make personal calls. For example, we may manufacture a wire stand to hold a reader's book at a proper angle for study. The item may retail for less than a dollar and it could be handled by every dealer in the country who sells stationery or reading matter. That would aggregate upwards of a million. The first step would be to refine the dealer-potential to stores selling textbooks. This qualification might reduce our list to approximately 7,500. Our first decision is not to attempt to secure personal representation to the market as a whole. But a letter here would be practical because once we had the names of the store owners, we would have our mailing list. Even the largest bookstores would not stand on ceremony if you overlooked a purchasing agent.

LOCATING STRATEGIC RECEIVERS AND MARKETS

A more typical problem for industrial selling is related to selling larger companies where the professional buyer is highly accessible but the strategic guy is invisible from the street. Or the marketing problem of small or medium size specialized producers of components or supplies that have a potential market in companies of all sizes. For example, a producer of metal stampings may be confined to a small geographic area and to a tight little group of users in one or two industries. His business may be slipping, for one reason or another, and he should seek new markets. Let us examine his possibilities.

LETTERS IN DIVERSIFICATION SITUATIONS

He probably is a reader of a half-dozen industrial magazines in his field. But his intentions do not change overnight from a few counties to the entire nation. Because industries are frequently concentrated in producing geographic areas, he probably is located in a metals working economy. His marketing limitation is that he has been confined to a small number of customers. If he is reaching substantially the entire market in his geographic division, he has few choices that do not include either diversification or changing locations. Without permitting our example to wander from the letter writing possibilities, let us simply assume that our troubled example decides to broaden his lines. He might add to his stamping business a franchise to supply a line of industrial fasteners. This is a fairly compatible addition. The advantage of adding such a supply line would be that the same purchasers he had been dealing with frequently also buy fasteners. Not infrequently these fasteners are attached to his stampings in, or prior to, assembly.

In such a diversification his initial prospects would be his present customers. But they already have fastener sources. That does not come as news to him, but he may learn that none is ready to consider him a fastener source soon. His problem is sticky. He and his representatives are well acquainted with the buyers, but the buyers know them as stamping, not fastener salesmen. Here is a situation that calls for a letter from president to president.

We should further qualify our stamper's entrance into fasteners by asserting that he found a line that promised savings. His representatives found that buyers did not doubt the savings, their objection was, mainly, "we are tooled for what we use and there is no chance of changing, at least not this year."

This is not an easy example to live with. A great many industrial products require lead-time of one, two or sometimes three years before changes can be engineered. But regardless of buyers' knowledge or attitudes, no design specifications get into any engineering until they are put there by engineers. So our stamping supplier who has been dealing with buyers for years is now beholden to engineers if he is to progress. But as we have observed earlier in this discussion, it is difficult to see who is responsible within companies and departments.

In situations such as proposed here, where the seller-buyer relationship is well established, great damage can result to the supplier if he "goes over the head" of the buyer. So he has a problem even before he composes a letter to anyone. He must face up to that by telling the buyer that his company would like to qualify as a fastener supplier. In cases such as this, it is a handicap if the supplier-company president is handling the account himself. If he is not, once his representative has advised the purchasing department, he can fire a letter to the president announcing his new identification.

ESTABLISHED SUPPLIER LETTERS TO PRESIDENTS—AVOID ENCLOSURES

Letters of established suppliers to presidents get outstanding attention even though they violate most rules. One rule that must not be violated is: do not include any enclosures. This must be adhered to even though your new line is highly photogenic. The remote exception is that the two officials are personal friends, but in that case no letter is necessary. Our letter makes its first mark that of identifying ourselves as a long-term supplier.

GETTING THE PURCHASING AGENT ON YOUR SIDE

Its second departure from the ordinary is that it shows: "copy to purchasing agent" and any other officer whose name might be expected. Placing those names on the letter to the president so that the P. A. sees them on his copy not only removes any resentment, but may put the P. A. on our side for the first time.

The letter must tell our entire proposition in its opening. For example:

> The changes in tooling and other production aspects have been a factor in our decision to broaden our lines to include industrial fasteners. As stamping suppliers to your production for many years, we have long felt that there is room for considerable cost reduction in both attachment method and product related to this assembly need. With that viewpoint, we have explored the industrial fastener field until we came upon a product, the ———— type fastener, that can effect savings up to 30 percent against standard industry costs. The adoption of this fastener would require some special tooling, taken into consideration in my estimate of net savings of 30 percent; and their adoption would be feasible only when other substantial engineering changes are being made. My purpose in writing is that I should like you to designate which engineer our chief engineer should work with to make necessary evaluations.
>
> The reason that this type of fastener has not previously been standardized in the industry is that. . . .

FOLLOWING-UP YOUR LETTER WITH APPOINTMENTS: WHO SEES WHO?

As we go into the body of that letter, we tell "how and why." In letters to company heads from top officers of suppliers it is always effective to ask, "Which executive should we see?" An interesting aspect of the answer you receive is that invariably the president names the vice president department head. That may be a trap if you plan to send a representative. That representative had better be your vice president of marketing. The customer vice president may agree to an appointment with anyone who calls after your letter to the president motivated him. But you either should go yourself (president) or send your vice president.

CHAPTER XVII

MOST BUSINESS LETTERS LACK PERSPECTIVE

Some Things To Avoid

If there are rules in letter writing they are made to be broken. Especially those we can do without. The letter, as the most personal of all written communications, must reflect its writer. There can be no absolute right or wrong way.

A recent examination of 1,000 letters, gathered at random in several large company offices, revealed the following tendencies: 80 percent were "one way" (selling) letters from strangers who revealed their purpose in the salutation or first paragraph; almost half opened with a question, real or rhetorical; and 200 showed stoppers, many in a second color, such as, "You Can Have Dinner Tonight In The Tropics."

Professionals in each field of business writing are aware that fads are a part of styles. Current styles in letters are in a wave of stoppers: "... 60% Profit ..."; "Everything is A-OK ..."; or, "... On the Hot Line." They are using talking animals, far-out slang and teenage "in" talk. These attention getters may be in the form of understatements, overstatements or non-sequiturs. There might be justification for these in some consumer letters, but we are considering those used in commercial and personal business letters. Today's avalanche of letters pouring into professional and business offices, addressed to corporate or division heads, to widely-known names and to investor and board members, offer a real challenge to letter writers. No one wants his material to die at the secretary's desk. Some are fighting it with screaming colors and designs on mail pieces, while others hope to get to the inner sanctum in a quieter way.

In suggesting or negating letter elements, our discussions deliberately deal extensively with smaller companies and lesser known organizations that use letters heavily. Although the preponderance of business mailings are to consumers (the next in number is the commercial type aimed at the departmental levels or to retail managers and owners), we devote great attention to reaching top level business and professional offices. Our reason for this emphasis is that the letter itself is of diminishing import in consumer mailings from larger companies, and its essentiality in commercial mailings is shrinking. So far no one has really solved the problem of reaching the top people. This closing discussion deals largely with some mistaken notions, and clears the ground for more effective courses.

GIMMICKS, CLICHÉS AND THE "FRIENDLY BIT" MUST GO

A clinical reader sees in attention-getters a deadly pattern of monotony—little telegrams saying, "PLEASE, PLEASE READ THIS LETTER!" They are meant to whet the curiosity, get attention, etc. In whatever form they appear, these gimmicks, clichés and "friendly bits" are not helping letters. We will enumerate some that must go. We will also discuss some elements and phrases to be avoided—those that are ". . . better left unsaid . . . ."

QUESTIONS, QUESTIONS, QUESTIONS

Do not start any letter with a question.

Your letter should say something, not ask something. If your letter reaches a responsible individual, he is entitled to see immediately what you want. It is largely a question of time. In self interest, state your business. Keep in mind that an executive whose secretary receives several hundred letters daily cannot physically pick up and read all of them. The same goes for purchasing agents, chief engineers, marketing directors and other executives. All of their names and titles are in numerous directories, and they appear on dozens of commercial and professional mailing lists.

AVOID USING COMMERCIAL LETTERHEADS TO TOP MEN

In spite of the traffic, some letters *do* reach corporate heads, physicians and specialized executives in the firing range of thousands of suppliers. Very few of these successes are written on two-color commercial letterheads that list their products. Your letter must first pass the secretary or staff assistant. Its best chance is to be unaccompanied, or with one enclosure of "quality" that matches the engraved executive stationery that you use.

NO STOPPERS, PLEASE

If your letter is in the hands of its addresee, the need for attention-getters is past. You need not ask, "How would you like to double your income?" Even when writing to middle management, or such presumed captives as civic executives, the rhetorical question stamps your offering as dubious. At best it may seem to be "the friendly bit."

OMIT CUTE OR WISE QUOTES

Of these several negative non-essentials to arouse curiosity or get attention, the cute saying is undoubtedly the deadliest. Here is an actual opening from an air conditioner manufacturer: "Everyone talks about the weather but no one does anything about it. That may have been true a century ago, but today something has been done about the weather. Seriously, we have a new indoor-outdoor thermometer reserved for you."

A moment's reflection upon that opening indicates that it is the result of complete subjectivity. Apparently the writer planned to attract attention with the cliché, and then quickly announce the gift offering. He started with a cumbersome sentence or two, and went on to squeeze it into the form shown.

SOME CONSUMER LETTERS HAVE LICENSE

Professional business letter writers know their markets. All of them have tests to determine techniques, forms and the presumed need for "attention-getters." Consumer letters have no problems capturing readers, but a travel agent's letter would get short shrift in a busy office, especially if it opened, "How would you like to spend this evening in Bali?" Yet as a householder, the busy-at-the-office executive might read it at home and dream. As an arouser, the romantic touch has a long history among travelers. The substantial travel market is well-identified by agencies. The Bali trip may not be for tonight, but for the travel market the question is literal. Book readers, credit users and countless types of hobbyists seem on the lookout for two, three and four page letters on their favorite subject. This partially reflects a joining urge, but even more it indicates a hunger for news of their hobby.

AVOID OVERWORKING YOUR LETTER

Do not expect a letter to sell more than one idea. Your reader is absorbed in his own affairs as he starts to read. If your proposition has appeal, it is because it jumped out at him as he started reading. To add a second thought would be changing the subject. Many letters begin, ". . . to acquaint you with our new line . . . ," and wind up with a coupon for a trial order. Keep the letter to its purpose. Do not enlarge your offering.

DO NOT "VISIT" IN BUSINESS LETTERS

Even when your *vis-à-vis* is a personal friend, your letter has a job to do. You must give it a chance. Your proposition must be strictly business. It requires the same justification. Avoid opening your letter with "personal stuff." Unless you both are sole owners of your companies, office-to-office business letters of the ". . . expect to be in your city . . ." type should be entirely business.

OMIT "GUESSING" PROSPECT'S VALUE

In writing personal business letters to "natural" prospects, it is easy to kindle resistance by assuming that the recipient wants your offer.

While "confident assumption" may be effective in personal selling, the vagaries of mood and other conditions of your reader require that you state your proposition without over-estimating your prospect's interest.

BE AWARE OF RECIPIENT'S SEX: MAN OR WOMAN?

In personal selling letters to business, most writers assume that the recipient is a man. In drafting consumer letters they assume a woman reader. The differences in motivation, attitudes and other conditions can be considerable. It is highly possible that a business woman is untouched by a letter aimed at a man. Where examination of clues leaves you uninformed, you address the letter to the preponderant sex. In writing to business women, address all as "Miss," unless you know your recipient is "Mrs." For general business use, all are "Mr.," until you can identify better. That also applies to consumers: all are "Mrs." When writing personalized letters, great attention must be given to titles. Clergy, court or government officials, military, and various types of doctors must be identified correctly.

"FLATTERY WILL GET YOU NO PLACE"

Unexplained praise or "flattering" references in business letters from strangers is well-meant but rarely helps effective letters. "Your standing in the business community . . ." is hardly impressive coming from a writer trying to sell something. These apparently trivial amenities in person-to-person meetings can be negative when put into letters.

THE PRICE IS PART OF THE PROPOSITION

In commercial letters soliciting orders, memberships or subscriptions that include a trial, no-money-now offer, do not avoid putting the price as close to or within the statement of the proposition itself. You must judge and plan the content of your offer that makes up your proposition. If the price (shown in payments or otherwise) makes the first paragraph burdensome, it should be put in the second paragraph as part of the justification. Keep in mind that if it's a good proposition, sent to the right addressee, the price is within their means.

Avoid the "friendly sound" at all costs, even when the letter goes to employees. Letters that sound friendly always sound weak. No amount of friendliness in a business letter, no matter how well it is written, can replace a good proposition and facts. Staff writers who compose letters for officers' signatures are often prone to "over-friendly" writing.

Do not insert personal reflections into the opening. Example: "We are introducing a new valve that has been long awaited, at least we have long awaited its production, and I am sure you . . . ." You cannot afford giving your opinion. The letter should say, "We are introducing a new valve designed to reduce a cost in installation and another in operation." Once you have said "increase profit" or "reduce cost," your reader is interested. This holds for commercial personalized letters. If it is sent to a top officer it should be on personalized engraved stationery.

Never make any reference to the reader's present method or product in the opening of any letter to a stranger, even if you know that the product he is currently using is out of date. When you know a prospect is having trouble with his present model, he also knows it.

Under no compulsion should you exaggerate at the beginning of your letter. Exaggeration and "humble pie" are equaly negative extremes in business letters.

We should take great care whenever we use such expressions as "your refrigerator problems," or "your tire problems." It might best be said, do not write "your problems." As those with selling experience know, the surest way to cause a prospect to defend his present method or product is to criticize it. When we attempt to visualize why our proposition might interest a reader, our aim should be to "meet his needs."

Never say, "at a very slight cost to you." Few people will buy a product or service that is introduced as costing anything. It must save money. That is the way the successful Cadillac salesmen approach prospects. All luxury items must "save." In letters it is not easy to say, "you are paying for it but not getting it," but that is the basic sales appeal for all quality products or services. However, that expression should be used sparingly if at all in letters. It is calculated to be offensive in direct selling, or even in advertising. But when you use such statements in letters you are criticizing his present method.

Never address a letter to the male head-of-household and tell him *anything* is good for, or pleasing to, his wife. Few men feel a need for such suggestions from strangers.

In consumer letters offering innovations to households, such as boats, power mowers or air coolers, avoid suggesting its value to any specific member of the family. In instances where "a benefit to the children" is mentioned, the product should be educational, or in some instances it may relate to health if it assumes that the child is now healthy.

AVOID APPEALS TO "HAVE MORE FUN"

Consumer letters must be extremely sparing in reference to pleasure or fun, even though they be sent to enroll a new member of a bowling league, country club or trip to Rome. To broaden the appeal of your letter, practical benefits should be placed ahead of pure fun. For example:

> Dear Mr. Jones:
>
> It is my pleasure to invite you to membership in a recreational bowling league being formed to meet the needs of business and professional men of our neighborhood whose schedules do not permit attendance on a given pre-determined evening each week. We would like to have you join us for a cocktail at the Lanes Red Room, Friday, September 8, where we will explore the time-preferences of those who would benefit from the indicated flexible schedule. If you can come, our informal meeting will start at 8:00 p.m.
>
> A year ago several of our busier neighbors whose business precludes "neighborhood commitments" formed a league with an arrangement permitting a second weekly date as optional to avoid conflicts. It worked out so well we are now going ahead with another group.
>
> Some weeks ago we informally surveyed some professional and business men in the neighborhood and learned that almost all considered bowling to be the winter exercise and recreational activity counterpart for summer's golf. That confirmed a fact we had learned after becoming interested in this healthy sport some years ago. Its original appeal to me was that no sizable cost in equipment or "membership" is involved. If you are not familiar with "neighbor-

hood business men bowling," please try to drop in next Friday. I am enclosing a return card to mark if we can expect you, or otherwise.

Best wishes until we meet,

    Sincerely yours,

    Joe Swift
    Manager
    Oaklyn Lanes

That letter omits the "pleasures" of bowling. Anyone who can not envision that is not a prospect. By omitting "pleasure" and stressing recreation, your prospect's wife will urge his consideration. The mention of golf opens the door to mentioning "no sizable cost." Without over-emphasizing time requirements, our letter is aimed at the limited time and money prospect.

As a first generation "big market" industry, bowling offers an excellent example of a business that needs the "personal implications" of personal business letters. It not only confined its growth to general recreation and novelty appeal, it has depended almost entirely upon "word of mouth" from its customers who prefer clublike exclusivity.

DO NOT DEPEND UPON YOUR CUSTOMERS

The "ask the man who owns one" idea has dwindled. He may have one because he likes crowds. "The place is always crowded," he enthuses. Bowling has a terrific market potential, but the fact that no one planned its transition in keeping with its plant expansion gives us at least one example of a consumer industry that has not shown guilt in adding to the mail avalanche. Letter writers should know that whenever they write for products or services that are highly visible but under-defined, that volunteer boosters may be killing sales. Always fully state your proposition and then justify it. Even the "fun cars" are advertised as efficient transportation.

OMIT "EVERYBODY'S DOING IT"

Just as services and products seeking "elevated status" are confining their markets ("everybody's buying one" may be good mass appeal), the personal business letter proposition should be based on inherent value—expected benefits. It's not for everyone, but it is for the man who wants better (recreation) at (sensible) prices. Bowling quickly gained "club identity" among its adherents, but its basic definition got lost. The value of business letters in cultivating its basic market (middle-age businessmen, middle-class) will be discovered when letter writers identify their market and determine what it wants.

DO NOT CONFUSE MARKET WITH MOTIVATION

Because bowling is in a slump (although undoubtedly it is destined to serve the nation's winter recreational needs on a footing equal to summer's golf), its present communications needs offer letter students excellent examples of techniques for semi-accepted products and services. Even as this industry's capacity increased far beyond its market development, marketing novices (operators) continued to shoot at their markets with scatter-guns. As TV and other glamour forms magnetized youth, they went after young families with teen agers and suburban families in the late '30's and early '40's who carried large mortgages. Both the young men and young family markets were available. But the older family, who really need this product's benefits and have the funds, was not in their plans. Glamour facilities for the young are a cash crop in suburbs because glamour is a motivation. The market is something else. If bowling's best market appeal is recreation, it should be defined for the middle-aged who need it.

AVOID TALKING ABOUT HEALTH

Health's part in marketing is confined to health products. Among the most conspicuous of these is in the travel field. But travel promoters need not mention "health." They describe their facilities and other attributes. In an age before sophicated marketing, health resorts and spas were the commodities available for those doing "poorly." When marketing sharpened to broaden its appeal the health-selling institutions faded.

The rule is: when people are ill they seldom invest in commodities not on the "doctor's orders" list. When they are well they aren't interested in "health."

DO NOT ANTICIPATE YOUR READER'S RESPONSE

Our suggestion that before preparing a letter you concentrate on the needs of your customer instead of on your product or service was aimed at reducing your subjectivity. In establishing a letter objective you must clearly identify the central need of your market as shown in age, sex, income, location and other factors. That must be handled very carefully because it has some aspects of "telling the other fellow about his business." When you have identified a central reason with broad applications for purchase of your product or service, adhere to it closely in shaping your proposition. If it misses the target, more market study may be needed.

NEVER ATTEMPT TO GUESS PRODUCT APPEAL

When a new product catches on friendly observers usually can "tell you why." Following such information can diminish your participation even as the market grows. You should set up ways and means of learning why families or individuals are buying. When you have that the specialized appeal of letters are well suited to purchases involving new definitions and steering on prices and uses.

DO NOT DEPEND ON LETTERS FOR NON-ACCEPTED PRODUCTS

Even though consumer mailings for "brand new Cleaner" or another packaged item appears to be offering a non-accepted product by mail, the fact is that women know each new "box" contains the same content. She may buy it to redeem the coupon for a quarter. If a product is really new, it should first be defined and shown in stores and in local media before letter selling. Similarly, personal business and commercial letters for new industrial products (non-accepted) should be confined to asking for sales appointments.

DO NOT OVERESTIMATE AN UNKNOWN COMPANY NAME

If your company cannot expect its brand or corporate name to be familiar, that fact should be included as part of your proposition.

Should your personal business letter get into the hands of a corporate official because it has a worthwhile appearance, he may be attracted to your proposition. But the fact that you are unknown to him can make him think the offer is aimed at smaller companies.

"As one of the smaller, highly specialized producers in the petrochemical field, we are . . ." tells him that he should not have expected to know you. In consumer mailings by "unknowns," a similar explanation should be made: "Although we are widely-known in the industrial and business fields, this marks the introduction of our first supermarket product in this territory. To quickly acquaint you . . . ."

OMIT MENTION OF HIGH QUALITY SERVICE

In letters offering services with indicated quality advantages, letter writers should avoid mention of cost in any form. For example, some city banks now solicit fur storage, usually on a limited basis. That type of service would be suited to the upper-income customer. The unexpected source of the service will not last too long. Your letter should put your case entirely on quality. For example, a bank offering fur storage in its vaults stresses preparation and quality.

> Dear Mrs. Jones:
>
> In keeping with our long practice of providing security in our vaults for valuables of our customers, we are now prepared to process and store your furs. In the belief that a superior fur storage involves proper advance preparation as well as proper temperatures and atmospheric conditions, we have engaged one of the fur industry's most expert fur handling authorities to supervise our service.
>
> We are not now issuing a public announcement of this customer service as our present plans are to invite only our regular customers to utilize the service. We are extending our vault services for these valuables because our directors were agreed that there is a need for a type of service not now offered by commercial establishments.
>
> If we can serve you, please mention it at any one of our offices; or, you may call this office. We will have our specialist call you to discuss arrangements.
>
> > Cordially yours,
> >
> > State Bank

When companies offering services for which their facilities may be limited, they should keep their offer to limited segments of the market, then expand. The author discussed its storage services with a bank vault operation who said that they had arranged with a wholesale furrier for preparing furs for storage. The letter shown here is almost identical with the single letter they used. Originally they had planned extending the offer through newspaper ads. In its first year the letter response brought almost capacity business at rates "approximately double commercial rates."

The letter shown is based on the bank's letter which was prepared by its advertising agency. They said, "It was meant to be very low-pressured." These letter writers were aware that families with substantial buying power seldom over-pay for anything even though money is not the first consideration for purchases related to a "quality" need. No enclosures went with the letter, nor were there any follow-up letters.

OMIT STANDARD SALES LITERATURE WITH ENGRAVED LETTERHEAD

The engraved executive stationery is often your best investment for entry into professional offices and on to executive's desks. To enclose your gaudiest folders compares to wearing your tan brogans with your dinner jacket. If selling the "top people" is involved in your marketing, do it right. Order your letter shop or printers to convert your product story onto a good letter-size engraved (processed) folder. If it requires 8 x 11 or other large size, send your letter without it, saying: "Under separate cover I am addressing to you a personal copy of our line-brochure . . . ." Your executive return cards also might well be on white stock.

DO NOT "CHANGE PACE" IN ACT NOW CLOSE

Among letters recently analyzed, a great many that were well-done in presenting an interesting proposition and justifying favorable response, suddenly took on a "fire sale" urgency in the close. It is always a temptation to add that adjective that gets faster action. The tempo and mood of your letters have considerable bearing on their effectiveness. One that is well modulated until its end, then shows overexcitement, loses all it has. Phrases like ". . . supplies are limited," or ". . . this offer will not be repeated," have a frantic sound. Adhere to your tone to the end.

AVOID THE ORIGINAL: EMBRACE THE FRESH BUT SIMPLE WAY

Among the most deceptive notions related to communications is the belief that originality makes propositions more effective. At this stage of the game, when business communications have matured through the great skills of thousands of organizations, it is not the time to look for "originality." If you should hit upon something original in technique, formula or your letter content, it would be highly unlikely to find a single understanding and responsive reader. Meanwhile, after we are reconciled to stating our story in a tried and true form, we should try to freshen it up and put into our most simple language.

Every minority with a cause or business segment with a product evolves its trade-talk language. This language invariably seeps to its customers and becomes familiar to the outsider. "Show biz" talk is part of an actor's life even though it may annoy others. Madison Avenue talk or Seventh Avenue talk may amuse their colleagues, but by the time it has general currency it is very tried and tiresome. Philosophers, government thinkers and scientists have languages that become public. Seldom are their words as easy to read as the simpler words they seem to oust.

Business letter language should be very simple. If it is really simple it will be fresh. At one time letters had a fantastic language of their own: "Y's R'cied, contents notd. . . ." In transition, this corn was considered comic. Disowning that, corn led to an "originality" urge. Our hope now is to get ourselves onto a simple language track. Long words are not under attack here. Always use the word that is best established with you. That will take care of "novelty" words and pomposities.

May we say in parting: If your business letter always says what you have in mind, your answers will be what *they* have in mind.

ABOUT THE AUTHOR

Patrick Monaghan has spent over 30 years developing his "psychology of selling." His first confrontation with the buying public was in his high school days. During the Great Depression in the early '30's, he supported his five children by selling products directly to the home and he also authored a salesman's training manual used by one of the nation's leading appliance manufacturers. Later in his career, Pat Monaghan was in charge of public relations for the Hotpoint division of General Electric. At the present time, he heads a public relations and merchandise consultant firm in New York. Some of the nation's largest consumer and industrial products manufacturers rely on him to effectively "sell" them to the public. One sales tool almost always suggested to his clients is the letter campaign. He considers a good sales letter one of the best "door-opening" devices around.